Southern Living

around the southern table

135 West 50th Street, New York, NY 10020

ISBN-13: 978-0-8487-3653-8
ISBN-10: 0-8487-3653-2
Library of Congress Control Number: 2012943004

Printed in the United States of America
First Printing 2012

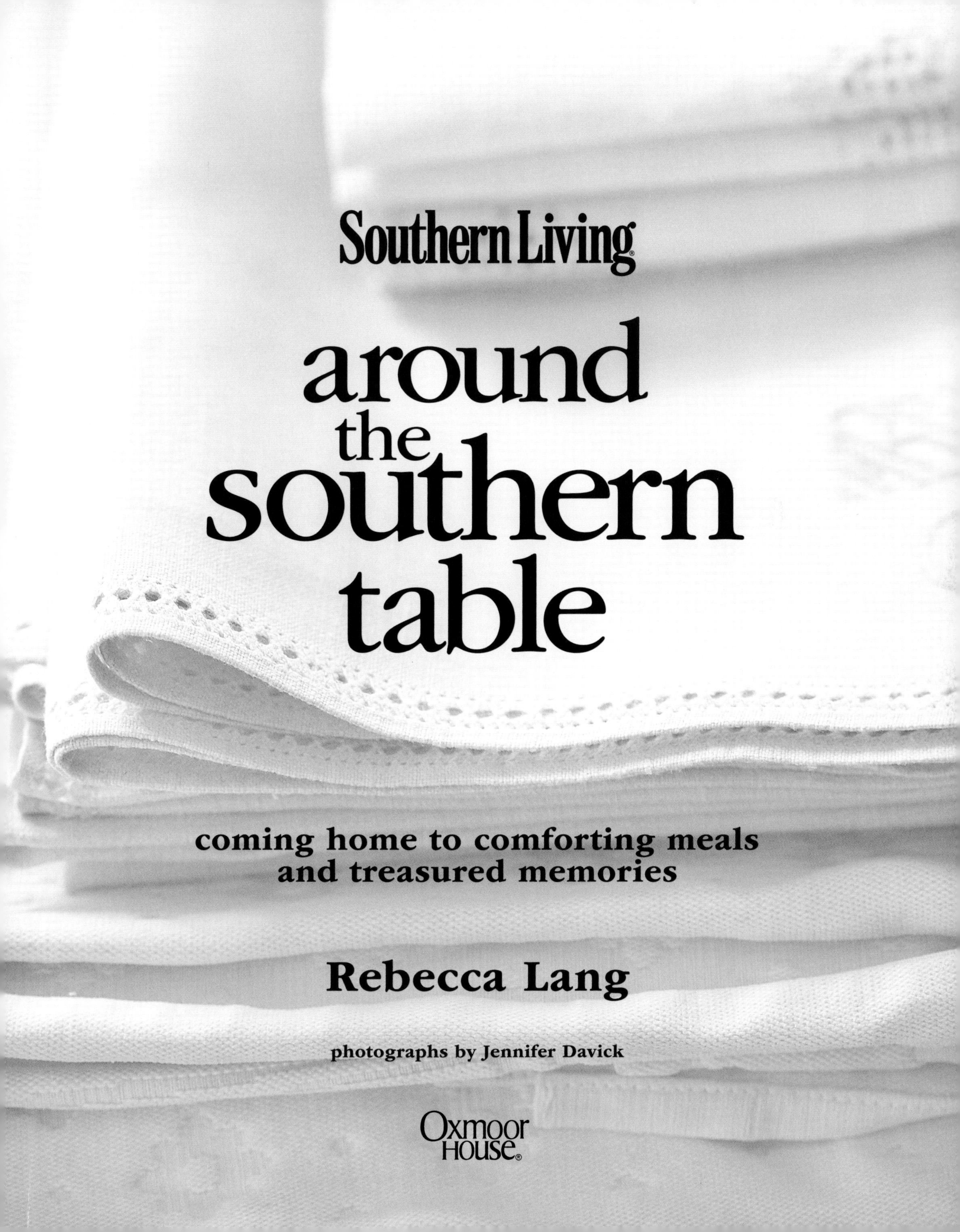

Southern Living

around the southern table

coming home to comforting meals and treasured memories

Rebecca Lang

photographs by Jennifer Davick

Oxmoor House

For Mama–

I love you for everything
you bring to my table.

contents

pull up a chair	8
sunup	16
little bites, sips & jars	46
dinner bell	86
from the oven	128
soup spoons & sliced bread	170
harvest time	200
sugar bowls	232
paper napkins & extra leaves	278
metric equivalents	283
index	284
bibliography	286
acknowledgments	287
about the author	288

foreword

Rebecca Lang's love of good food has been evident to me since we met more than 15 years ago. She was a young student at the University of Georgia when she first contacted me about apprenticing. I was skeptical, as she lived about an hour away. She arrived cheerfully and on time, with talent and enthusiasm for cooking and a passion for teaching from the very start.

Although she went on to study French techniques at Johnson & Wales University, Rebecca's love of her family's Southern food never left her. Her grandmother, Tom, was part of this inspiration. A woman who always had a biscuit bowl and an iron skillet at the ready, Tom could cook anything Southern, it seemed, and make it exceptional. One day when Rebecca and Tom visited me, Tom cooked her tender, fluffy biscuits with ease, even at 97 years old. Rebecca and I learned anew that techniques are as important in Southern cooking as in any other cuisine and should be captured and passed on to future generations.

Memories of Tom's table—plus techniques and recipes Rebecca learned working with *Southern Living,* writing cookbooks, teaching, and appearing on television—make her an authority on Southern food. Her expertise in the kitchen, her warmth at the table, and her love of cooking for her family and others are evident in this book. As you prepare the recipes on these pages, you are sure to find and share in Rebecca's love for honest Southern food, just as her grandmother and I did so long ago.

Nathalie Dupree

Author of 12 cookbooks about the American South,
including *Mastering the Art of Southern Cooking*

pull up a chair

an invitation to the comfort, warmth, and beauty of the southern table

I was a girl fascinated by biscuits, fried chicken, and pound cake. In the small Georgia town where I grew up, cooking was a way of life. With the pocket of my grandmother's apron at eye level, I discovered that the best place for snacks was close to the counter—and that the kitchen was where I belonged.

I always feel at peace when I cook, and I am happiest when I'm serving those I love around our treasured dining room table (pictured at right).

This antique oak oval is the same table where my cherished grandmother Tom and her 10 siblings ate when they were small, like my own children are now. It has eight leaves, though we usually use just one or two, and it comfortably seats up to 10. At any given time, it may be piled high with everyday flatware, sippy cups, and crayons, or set with my favorite white linen napkins and finest china. Family meetings, comforting meals, morning coffee, and homework all happen here.

I suspect neither my career nor this book would exist if not for this beloved piece of furniture. It's where generations learned to climb up to their plates—and where I developed a deep love for the food, hospitality, and people of the South. The table is the destination for each and every recipe I make. It's where, even in a house filled with the sound of little feet running from room to room, we all still routinely stop to eat and enjoy our time with each other.

We connect at the table, pray at the table, and solidify our relationships each time we pull up a chair.

Rebecca Lang

southern hospitality: how we do

The tea is always sweet, the screen door is never latched, and the warm greeting comes with a Southern drawl. There is an air of welcoming in the South not found any other place on Earth. Behind each "yes, ma'am" and every buttered biscuit, there's an unmistakable feeling that can't be bottled or sold.

This uniquely Southern sense of hospitality extends to the comforting ingredients that make our food our own. Whether it's creamy grits or fried okra, a plate of satisfying Southern food makes anyone feel at home. At the first glimpse of a moving truck, we hit the kitchen to whip up homemade pound cakes for new neighbors. We have learned the delicate art of keeping warm casserole dishes level on our laps on the way to covered-dish suppers. Sharing something from the kitchen is the way we say, "Welcome."

It's not just about food; it's in all we do. It's writing a sweet thank-you note on real paper or taking supper to a neighbor in need. It's waving at every car that passes, even when we don't recognize the driver. Men hold doors open for women, and preachers know who's sitting in the pews. A friend is always ready to lend a hand, and the wine is chilled and ready.

Maybe it's the cast-iron skillets of cobbler and the plates of crisp fried chicken that make it such an easy place to love. Maybe it's the generosity of those who call it home. Either way, the South stands apart as a place where there is always room for another plate, another chair, or another new friend at the table.

dining room tables: so much more than furniture

Tables are not just resting places for plates and glasses. They are anchors, touchstones, and centerpieces for so much of life in the South.

Many Southerners have grown up, loved, laughed, prayed, and experienced the truest sense of home around the table. Though the table and its location change, those who surround it are always family. Being welcomed at the table is a priceless gift, an unspoken assurance that you are not alone.

In times of great celebration, quiet reflection, or deep loss, the table is the hub, the heart, the center so many return to. It's where we welcome friends, address wedding invitations and baby announcements, write thank-you notes, complete homework, study Bibles, and organize bake sales.

I was blessed to inherit a magnificent dining room table from my grandmother Tom. This sacred piece of furniture has been the pillar of my family since long before I was born. Tom grew up eating her meals at the very same table. By the time it came to me, my great grandparents had raised 11 children around it, and it needed some TLC. I refinished the oak, re-covered the chair seats, and fell in love with it all over again. I can only hope that my grandchildren follow our family legacy of honoring the table and its history.

No matter the age of your table and the stories it could tell, it remains a place to forget distractions, put away technology, and enjoy every minute with those you love.

vintage tabletop pieces: history you can touch

In the South, the items that dress the table tie us to our history as much as the recipes themselves. Handing down table linens from generation to generation is a right of passage for Southern women. As the years pass, a new holiday hostess in the family takes in all the relatives, the recipes, and, if she is lucky, a coveted stack of linens. Some have monograms from someone she never knew, some are stained and creased with priceless character, and some have witnessed meals that lasted for hours. Pulling out and using vintage family linens is paying homage to those who came before you.

Even if they are not from your family, old china, glassware, and specialized serving pieces—such as deviled egg plates, cake stands, sweet tea pitchers, slotted spoons, and turkey platters—bring a sense of the past to everyday meals. I've always thought of silverware as being incredibly personal, chosen carefully by others during a pivotal time of their lives. To look over the patterns that now reside with me gives me a glance into weddings long before I was born.

Combining heirloom and modern pieces adds personality and style to any table. From lace to oilcloth, vintage Southern linens make fabulous conversation pieces. Because sizes vary, you may need to layer different shapes and colors of linens to achieve the ideal overhang, but this only adds to the character they bring. To keep linens in the best shape for years to come, wash and press them after each use, layer them with acid-free paper, and store them flat or rolled (to avoid folds) around a cardboard tube.

sunup

breakfast and brunch recipes for early risers and sleepy weekends

cheddar scrambled eggs (pictured on pages 16-17)

There are a few simple steps to really good scrambled eggs. Adding cream to the eggs makes them smooth and rich. Constant motion in the pan makes them fluffy. Using fresh organic eggs and high-quality Cheddar guarantees a sunny color, perfect for starting the day.

8 large organic eggs
2 Tbsp. heavy cream
½ tsp. salt
¼ tsp. freshly ground pepper
2 oz. extra-sharp Cheddar cheese, shredded (½ cup)
1 Tbsp. unsalted butter

1. Whisk together first 4 ingredients. Stir in cheese.
2. Melt butter in a large nonstick skillet over medium heat; add egg mixture. Push eggs around skillet using a heatproof rubber spatula 4 to 5 minutes or until eggs are thickened but still moist. Remove from heat, season with more salt and freshly ground pepper to taste, and serve immediately.
Makes: 4 servings   Hands-on Time: 10 min.   Total Time: 10 min.

country ham with redeye gravy (pictured on pages 16-17)

On breakfast tables in some parts of the South, country ham with redeye gravy is just about as common as bacon. The origin of the name is debated, but the most common belief is that the gravy—a very thin, salty sauce—takes on a reddish tone from the browned bits scraped from the bottom of the skillet. Some Southerners make their gravy with water, others with coffee or cola. I use a mixture of cola and water to balance the salt and add sweetness and caffeine. When it comes to waking up, I usually need all the help I can get.

1 lb. country ham, cut into 3- x 4-inch pieces
2 Tbsp. unsalted butter
1½ cups cola soft drink

1. Cook ham, in 3 batches, in a large stainless-steel skillet (do not use nonstick) over medium heat 4 to 5 minutes on each side or until browned. (The skillet will be dry.) Remove ham from skillet.
2. Melt butter in skillet. Stir in cola and ½ cup water, and simmer 3 minutes, stirring with a spatula to loosen particles from bottom of skillet. Serve hot gravy with ham.
Makes: 6 servings   Hands-on Time: 20 min.   Total Time: 20 min.

country ham jam (pictured on pages 16-17)

Three strong Southern flavors—bourbon, country ham, and cola—come together in this rich, spreadable condiment. Slather it on biscuits or toast, and serve with scrambled eggs to start the day. Or use it to add Southern oomph to cheese and crackers at cocktail hour.

1 lb. country ham, finely chopped (about 3 cups)
2 cups chopped Vidalia onion
5 garlic cloves, minced
½ cup firmly packed light brown sugar
1 cup cola soft drink, divided
1 Tbsp. plus 2 tsp. cider vinegar
1 tsp. dried thyme
2 Tbsp. unsalted butter
1 Tbsp. bourbon
½ tsp. freshly ground pepper

1. Cook ham in a large skillet over medium heat 3 minutes, stirring occasionally. Add onion and garlic, and sauté 5 minutes or until onions are tender. Add brown sugar, and stir to coat ham. Add ½ cup cola soft drink and next 2 ingredients. Bring to a boil, reduce heat to low, and simmer, stirring occasionally, 30 minutes. (If mixture gets too dry, add 1 Tbsp. water.)
2. Add remaining ½ cup cola soft drink, and simmer 30 minutes, stirring occasionally. Remove from heat. Stir in butter and remaining ingredients. Cool 20 minutes.
3. Pulse mixture in a food processor 3 to 4 times or until ham is finely chopped and mixture is spreadable. Serve immediately, or store in an airtight container in refrigerator up to 1 week.

Makes: 2 cups Hands-on Time: 25 min. Total Time: 1 hr., 50 min.

signature pieces:
sugar bowl & creamer
On tables since the colonies were formed, these famous dishes hold two of the most popular ingredients in the South. Sugar bowls can be made with or without handles or lids. Spoons for scooping the sugar or tiny tongs for choosing cubes are kept in the bowls and should never be used to stir hot liquids. Some creamers are designed to keep in the refrigerator so chilled cream is always ready.

The sets come in endless shapes, sizes, and materials, and range widely in price. Creamers and sugar bowls should only be used together and most often are put to use during coffee or tea service. The pair may be passed during service or simply set near the coffee station.

breakfast in a skillet

The best of breakfast comes together here in a big cast-iron skillet. It's lovely enough to take straight from the oven to the table, even for company. Starting out the day this way sets a pretty high standard for lunch and supper. Preheating the skillet helps the biscuit crumbs stay crisp.

- 1 lb. ground pork sausage
- 1 cup diced onion
- 2 garlic cloves, minced
- 2 cups crumbled Cat-head Biscuits (page 159) or other homemade biscuits
- 6 oz. extra-sharp Cheddar cheese, freshly grated (1½ cups)
- 1 cup grape tomatoes, quartered
- ⅛ tsp. freshly ground pepper
- 6 large eggs

1. Preheat oven to 350°. Heat a 10-inch cast-iron skillet in oven 5 minutes.
2. Meanwhile, cook sausage, onion, and garlic in a large, lightly greased skillet over medium heat, stirring frequently, 10 minutes or until sausage is browned and onion is tender. Transfer to a large bowl. Add biscuit crumbles and next 3 ingredients. Stir until blended. Transfer to hot cast-iron skillet.
3. Make 6 indentations in sausage mixture using back of a spoon. Break 1 egg into each indentation.
4. Bake at 350° for 23 to 25 minutes or just until eggs are set. Serve immediately.
Makes: 6 servings   Hands-on Time: 20 min.
Total Time: 45 min., not including Cat-head Biscuits

pound cake french toast

Who says French toast has to be made with toast? At our house, we make it even more indulgent with leftover pound cake. Unlike traditional French toast, this decadent version needs no syrup or powdered sugar.

3 large eggs
¼ cup milk
¼ tsp. ground cinnamon
8 (¾-inch-thick) slices Pound Cake from Heaven (page 243)
Garnishes: fresh berries, whipped cream

1. Whisk together first 3 ingredients in a shallow dish or pie plate. Quickly dip cake slices, 1 at a time, into egg mixture, coating both sides.
2. Cook cake, in batches, on a nonstick griddle over medium heat 2 to 3 minutes on each side or until batter is golden brown and no longer wet. Garnish, if desired.
Makes: 8 servings Hands-on Time: 20 min.
Total Time: 20 min., not including pound cake

sweet candied bacon

Coating bacon with brown sugar turns a breakfast staple into a dreamy, can't-eat-just-one morning splurge. The edges crisp up, and the centers are pure candied goodness. Caution: Cooking bacon in the oven can generate a little smoke. Turn on the hood, or open the kitchen window, if needed.

½ cup firmly packed light brown sugar
2 Tbsp. balsamic vinegar
1 tsp. molasses
¼ tsp. ground red pepper
Cooking spray
1 (16-oz.) package bacon slices

1. Preheat oven to 400°. Stir together first 4 ingredients in a small bowl.
2. Line 2 jelly-roll pans with aluminum foil. Place ovenproof wire racks on foil in pans. Lightly coat with cooking spray. Arrange bacon in a single layer on racks. Brush top of bacon slices generously with brown sugar mixture using a pastry brush.
3. Bake at 400° for 28 to 30 minutes or until edges are crisp. Do not turn or flip. Bacon will look dark but will not be burned. Transfer from wire racks to a serving plate while bacon is still warm (to prevent sticking). Cool slightly before serving.
Makes: 4 to 6 servings Hands-on Time: 10 min. Total Time: 38 min.

southern staple: bacon drippings

On my grandmother's counter sat a small metal can containing the all-important liquid gold of the South: bacon drippings. The can stayed far from the fridge, and its pure, glorified contents were spooned out for everything from making cornbread and biscuits to greasing skillets and pans. The can was never empty because bacon was on the stove most mornings, and the drippings were replenished about as fast as they were used.

For generations, similar containers have been found on the backs of stoves all over the South. Like good cooks everywhere, Southerners know not to waste anything in the kitchen. Bacon drippings are a flavorful replacement for oil and butter, and if you cook with bacon as much as we do, you're bound to have some drippings on hand.

In my own kitchen, I save every single drop of rendered bacon fat. After cooking bacon, I remove the crisp pieces of meat from the pan and allow the drippings to cool slightly. (If they cool too long, they solidify.) I carefully pour the warm drippings into whatever clean glass jar is handy. Then I cover and store them in the refrigerator, which keeps the drippings fresh for months.

The amount of drippings rendered depends on the amount of fat in the bacon you cook and whether you have thick slices or thin. On average, two to three slices of bacon will generate one tablespoon of drippings.

The flavor is irreplaceable. That's why, at any given time, I have at least two full jars of bacon drippings in my fridge. Anytime I need a smoky, meaty boost in a recipe, the solution is just a spoonful away. However, should you find your drippings jar empty, you can make do with an equal amount of vegetable oil.

over-the-top egg sandwiches

Most Sunday nights when I was growing up, my dad made fried egg sandwiches. All these years later, Sunday sundowns often find me craving fried eggs and good bread. This layered knife-and-fork version is big, hearty, and just as good for breakfast as it is for supper.

12 oz. ground pork sausage
8 (½-inch-thick) slices sourdough bread
¼ cup unsalted butter, softened
1 Tbsp. extra virgin olive oil, divided
8 large eggs
Salt and freshly ground pepper
2 cups loosely packed baby arugula
1 large tomato, peeled (optional), and cut into ¼-inch-thick slices

1. Shape sausage into 4 patties about ¾ inch thick and roughly the same shape as your bread slices. Cook sausage patties in a 12-inch skillet over medium-low heat 7 minutes on each side or until centers are no longer pink and edges are crisp and browned. Drain on paper towels.
2. Meanwhile, toast the bread, and butter 1 side of each slice.
3. Heat 1½ tsp. oil in a clean nonstick skillet over medium-low heat, swirling skillet to coat bottom of skillet completely. Crack 2 eggs into skillet, and fry 4 to 6 minutes or until whites are completely set and yolks are nearly set. Sprinkle eggs with salt and pepper. Flip gently, and fry until yolk is just set (no more than 30 seconds). Transfer eggs to a plate. Repeat procedure 3 more times with remaining 6 eggs, oil, salt, and pepper.
4. Divide arugula among 4 bread slices, buttered sides up. Top each with some tomato slices, 1 fried egg, 1 sausage patty, and another fried egg. Top with remaining bread slices, buttered sides down. Serve immediately.
Makes: 4 servings Hands-on Time: 50 min. Total Time: 50 min.

sausage and cheese soufflé

This decadent morning meal chills overnight, so it's ready to bake even before you've had your first cup of coffee. Serve it right out of the oven when it's hot and bubbly.

1 lb. ground pork sausage
4 oz. extra-sharp Cheddar cheese
8 large eggs
2 cups milk
¾ tsp. salt
½ tsp. dried oregano
½ tsp. Dijon mustard
¼ tsp. freshly ground black pepper
⅛ tsp. ground red pepper
1 lb. croissants (about 20 medium), cut into 1-inch cubes
Garnish: minced fresh chives

1. Brown sausage in a large skillet over medium heat, stirring often, 10 to 13 minutes or until meat crumbles and is no longer pink. Drain and pat dry with paper towels.
2. Grate cheese on the large holes of a box grater.
3. Whisk together eggs and next 6 ingredients in a large bowl. Stir in croissant cubes. Add sausage and cheese; stir well. Pour into a lightly greased 13- x 9-inch baking dish. Cover and chill 8 to 24 hours.
4. Preheat oven to 350°. Remove dish from refrigerator, and let dish stand at room temperature while oven preheats. Bake, uncovered, at 350° for 55 minutes or until set. Garnish, if desired. Serve immediately.
Makes: 8 servings   Hands-on Time: 20 min.   Total Time: 9 hr., 15 min.

apple-glazed sausages and vidalias

The apple juice in this morning-time side dish creates a sweet glaze for the spicy sausages. Make the rest of the meal as the sausage cooks for a lazy weekend breakfast.

1½ lb. mild Italian sausage
2 Tbsp. extra virgin olive oil
1 Vidalia onion, thinly sliced (about 2 cups)
1 cup apple juice
¼ tsp. freshly ground pepper
½ tsp. finely chopped fresh rosemary

1. Cook sausage in hot oil in a large skillet over medium heat 8 minutes or until browned on all sides. Remove from skillet. Cut each sausage into 3 equal pieces (1½ to 2 inches each).
2. Add onion to skillet, and sauté 10 minutes or until soft. Return sausage to skillet. Stir in apple juice. Cover and cook 10 minutes.
3. Uncover, stir in pepper, and cook 5 minutes or until liquid has reduced and glazes sausage and onion. Remove from heat. Stir in rosemary. Serve immediately.
Makes: 4 to 6 servings Hands-on Time: 35 min. Total Time: 45 min.

stone-ground grits with homemade basil butter

People who say they don't like grits have simply tasted bad grits. Grits need to be cooked until no crunchiness remains; good ones don't require chewing. I like mine with herbed butter, which you can make with fresh basil and over-whipped cream.

1 cup uncooked stone-ground grits
2½ cups milk
1 tsp. salt
6 Tbsp. Homemade Basil Butter

1. Place grits in a bowl; add enough water to cover grits by about 1 inch. Skim off and discard any debris that floats to the top. Drain; transfer grits to a Dutch oven. Add milk, salt, and 3½ cups water.
2. Bring to a boil, reduce heat, and simmer, whisking often, 1 hour and 20 minutes or until grits are creamy and no longer crunchy. (If grits become too thick, whisk in more water.) Serve with Homemade Basil Butter.
Makes: 6 servings Hands-on Time: 15 min.
Total Time: 1 hr., 45 min., including butter

homemade basil butter

2 cups heavy cream
10 fresh basil leaves, thinly sliced
⅛ tsp. salt

1. Process cream in a food processor until liquid separates from solids (3 to 4 minutes). Remove solid cream, and pat dry with paper towels. Discard liquid. Clean and dry food processor bowl.
2. Return solid cream to processor. Add remaining ingredients. Process 10 seconds or until blended. Store in an airtight container in refrigerator up to 1 week.
Makes: 1 cup Hands-on Time: 10 min. Total Time: 10 min.

puffy grits

Few things are prettier than a puffed soufflé emerging from the oven. Race to the table so each guest can take in the glorious grits suspended in aged Parmigiano-Reggiano cheese. For this dish, I like to grate the cheese on the small holes of a box grater.

1 cup uncooked stone-ground grits (such as McEwen & Sons organic grits)
1 Tbsp. freshly grated Parmigiano-Reggiano cheese
4 large eggs, separated
2 cups freshly grated Parmigiano-Reggiano cheese
1 Tbsp. unsalted butter
1 tsp. Dijon mustard
¾ tsp. salt
⅛ tsp. freshly ground pepper

1. Place grits in a bowl; add enough water to cover grits by about 1 inch. Skim off and discard any debris that floats to the top. Drain; transfer grits to a Dutch oven. Add 5 cups water.
2. Bring to a boil, reduce heat, and simmer, whisking very often, until grits are creamy and tender, about 1 hour and 10 minutes. (If grits become dry and begin to stick before they are creamy, add more water, 2 Tbsp. at a time, and continue to cook until grits are tender.)
3. Preheat oven to 400°. Lightly grease a 1½-qt. soufflé dish. Sprinkle sides and bottom with 1 Tbsp. Parmigiano-Reggiano cheese.
4. Remove grits from heat, and transfer to a large bowl. Stir in egg yolks, 2 cups Parmigiano-Reggiano cheese, and next 4 ingredients.
5. Beat egg whites at high speed with an electric mixer until soft peaks form. Fold egg whites into grits mixture. Pour into prepared soufflé dish.
6. Bake at 400° for 50 to 55 minutes or until puffed and lightly browned. Serve immediately.

Makes: 6 servings   Hands-on Time: 15 min.   Total Time: 2 hr., 25 min.

table talk:
breakfast table

Often nestled in the kitchen or nearby, breakfast tables are smaller and more casual than formal dining tables. Some old Southern homes have breakfast rooms right off the kitchen. Not only is this designated room home to the breakfast table, but it's also a comfortable spot to share a meal while not being too far from the stove.

Such tables may have been intended just for morning coffee, but many families enjoy casual meals throughout the day at the breakfast table, a cozy spot that endures in the South.

buttermilk and brown sugar waffles

When the waffle iron is out on the counter, I can guarantee my children are in the kitchen squirming with excitement. It's almost as if they are willing the waffles to cook faster. I freeze any leftover waffles to liven up a weekday breakfast. They reheat nicely in the toaster.

2 cups all-purpose flour
3 Tbsp. light brown sugar
1 tsp. baking powder
½ tsp. salt
¼ tsp. baking soda
2 large eggs
¾ cup buttermilk
¾ cup milk
⅓ cup unsalted butter, melted
Garnishes: butter, syrup, blueberries

1. Whisk together first 5 ingredients in a large bowl.
2. Whisk together eggs and next 2 ingredients in a medium bowl. Add to flour mixture, and whisk just until blended. Whisk in melted butter.
3. Cook batter, in batches, in a preheated, oiled Belgian-style waffle iron until golden. (Cook times will vary.) Garnish, if desired.

Makes: 12 (4-inch) waffles Hands-on Time: 15 min. Total Time: 25 min.

ginger and peach muffins

Homemade peach preserves and crystallized ginger combine to make these muffins incredibly moist and satisfying. To bake each and every one perfectly, make sure every muffin cup gets some of the flavorful ginger-peach mixture. Use a large muffin pan, and fill each cup completely full of batter. If you have any leftover ginger-peach preserves, try mixing it with Champagne for a memorable cocktail.

3¼ cups peeled, chopped fresh peaches (2½ to 3 lb.)
¾ cup granulated sugar
½ cup chopped crystallized ginger
1 Tbsp. fresh lemon juice
2¼ cups all-purpose flour
1 Tbsp. baking powder
1 tsp. salt
1 tsp. ground cinnamon
¼ tsp. freshly grated nutmeg
3 large eggs, lightly beaten
1 cup milk
⅓ cup firmly packed light brown sugar
5 Tbsp. unsalted butter, melted
1 tsp. vanilla extract

1. Bring first 4 ingredients to a boil in a medium saucepan, stirring gently. Reduce heat, and simmer 20 minutes or just until peaches are tender and syrup is thick. Remove from heat, and cool completely (about 45 minutes). Reserve 2¾ cups mixture; set aside any remaining for another use.
2. Preheat oven to 400°. Whisk together flour and next 4 ingredients in a large bowl. Combine eggs and next 4 ingredients in a small bowl. Add to flour mixture, whisking just until dry ingredients are moistened. Add reserved peach mixture, and stir just until blended. (Batter will be lumpy.)
3. Stirring between scoops and scooping from the bottom of the bowl (to ensure each scoop has plenty of peach pieces), spoon batter into lightly greased (½-cup) muffin pans, filling each of 14 cups completely full.
4. Bake at 400° for 30 minutes. Cool in pans on wire racks 10 minutes; remove from pans to wire racks, and cool completely (about 45 minutes).
Makes: 14 muffins Hands-on Time: 25 min. Total Time: 3 hr.

brown-butter coffee cake with peaches and blueberries

Coffee cakes don't get any more inviting than this one. With luscious fruit and a nutty streusel topping, it's perfect for special occasions or relaxing weekends with company. Make it the night before so you and your guests can sleep in.

streusel

1 cup pecan halves
½ cup all-purpose soft-wheat flour (such as White Lily)
¼ cup granulated sugar
¼ cup firmly packed light brown sugar
¼ cup cold unsalted butter, cut into cubes
¼ tsp. salt

coffee cake

1 cup plus 2 Tbsp. unsalted butter
3 fresh peaches (about 1 lb.)
2 cups all-purpose soft-wheat flour
1 tsp. baking powder
½ tsp. salt
½ cup granulated sugar
½ cup firmly packed light brown sugar
4 large eggs
1 tsp. vanilla extract
1½ cups fresh blueberries, divided

1. Prepare Streusel: Pulse all 6 ingredients in a food processor 4 to 5 times or until pecans are chopped into ½-inch pieces. Transfer to a small bowl, and chill.
2. Prepare Coffee Cake: Cook butter in a wide heavy skillet over medium-low heat, stirring occasionally with a wooden spoon, 15 minutes or until butter begins to turn brown. Immediately remove from heat, and transfer to a shallow bowl. (Butter will continue to darken if left in skillet.) Cover and freeze until just congealed (about 20 minutes).
3. Preheat oven to 325°. Peel peaches, and cut each into quarters, discarding pits. Whisk together flour and next 2 ingredients in a medium bowl.
4. Beat chilled browned butter, granulated sugar, and brown sugar at medium speed with an electric mixer until fluffy (about 1 minute). Add eggs, 1 at a time, beating well after each addition. Add vanilla. Reduce speed to low, and gradually add flour mixture. Beat just until blended. Gently stir in 1 cup blueberries.
5. Pour batter into a greased and floured 10-inch springform pan. Arrange peach quarters in a circle on top of batter; place any remaining quarters in center of circle. Top peaches with streusel and remaining ½ cup blueberries.
6. Bake at 325° for 1 hour and 45 minutes or until a long wooden pick inserted in center comes out clean. Cool completely in pan on a wire rack (about 1 hour). Run a knife around outer edge of pan to loosen cake. Gently remove sides of pan. Cut cake into wedges, and serve.

Makes: 12 servings Hands-on Time: 36 min. Total Time: 3 hr., 21 min.

honey-pecan coffee cake

Easy to put together first thing in the morning, this coffee cake fills the kitchen with the scent of pecans, honey, cinnamon, and brown sugar. Raisins, plus a drizzle of white icing, bring back memories of old-fashioned cinnamon rolls.

batter

¾ cup granulated sugar
½ cup honey
½ cup unsalted butter, softened
2 large eggs
1 tsp. vanilla extract
2 cups self-rising soft-wheat flour (such as White Lily)
1 cup sour cream

topping

½ cup firmly packed light brown sugar
¼ cup unsalted butter, softened
2 Tbsp. self-rising soft-wheat flour
2 tsp. ground cinnamon
1½ cups pecan halves
½ cup raisins

icing

½ cup powdered sugar
4 tsp. milk
¼ tsp. vanilla extract

1. Preheat oven to 350°. Lightly grease a 9-inch square pan.
2. Prepare Batter: Beat granulated sugar, honey, and butter at medium-high speed with an electric mixer 3 minutes or until light and fluffy. Beat in eggs and vanilla. Add flour alternately with sour cream, beginning and ending with flour; beat well after each addition. Pour batter into prepared pan.
3. Prepare Topping: Pulse brown sugar and next 3 ingredients in a food processor 5 times or until mixture resembles coarse crumbs. Transfer to a bowl; stir in pecans and raisins until coated. Sprinkle mixture over batter. (Mixture will sink into cake as it bakes.)
4. Bake at 350° for 55 minutes or until a wooden pick inserted in center comes out clean. Let cool 30 minutes in pan on a wire rack.
5. Prepare Icing: Stir together all 3 ingredients in a small bowl. Drizzle icing over warm cake. Cut into squares. Serve warm.
Makes: 9 servings **Hands-on Time: 20 min.** **Total Time: 1 hr., 45 min.**

beignets with buttermilk

After my first trip to New Orleans, I woke up at night craving beignets. The sweet puffed pastries stayed in my mind much longer than other aspects of my adventure. Though they are typically served with breakfast or brunch, I also enjoy them later in the day. This buttermilk-and-yeast version, delicious with coffee and perfect for sharing with neighbors, makes enough for breakfast, afternoon snacks, and dessert.

1 (¼-oz.) envelope active dry yeast
½ cup warm water (105° to 115°)
½ cup granulated sugar, divided
1 cup milk
1 cup buttermilk
2 large eggs, lightly beaten
1 tsp. salt
3 Tbsp. unsalted butter, melted
6½ cups bread flour
Peanut oil
Sifted powdered sugar

1. Combine yeast, warm water, and 1 tsp. granulated sugar in bowl of a heavy-duty electric stand mixer; let stand 5 minutes. Add milk, next 3 ingredients, and remaining granulated sugar, beating at low speed until combined. Add melted butter, beating at medium speed until blended.
2. Gradually add 4 cups flour, beating at low speed after each addition until smooth. Gradually add remaining 2½ cups flour, beating until a sticky dough forms. Transfer to a lightly greased bowl, turning to grease top. Cover, and chill 6 to 24 hours.
3. Turn dough out onto a lightly floured surface; roll to ¼-inch thickness. Cut dough into 2½-inch squares using a pizza cutter or sharp knife.
4. Pour oil to depth of 2 inches into a Dutch oven; heat to 375°. Fry dough, in batches, turning often, 2 to 3 minutes or until golden brown. Drain on a wire rack. Immediately dust liberally with powdered sugar.
Makes: about 5 dozen **Hands-on Time: 1 hr.** **Total Time: 7 hr., 5 min.**

my southern table

I grew up on my family's peanut farm, which I now see as a privileged existence, even more so than being raised in a manor house with a governess and uniformed servants. It saddens me to see the family farm disappearing from the Southern landscape. Such a loss will cost us many things, but the rituals of the table might well be the most irreplaceable. As a farm family, we raised everything that appeared on our table.

Of course I didn't appreciate this lifestyle growing up in rural Alabama, nor did I consider it even remotely privileged. I longed for store-bought food—hot dogs, canned sauerkraut, and Hostess cupcakes—like city folks had. Instead, I got off the school bus in the afternoons and went to work for my supper. On the King farm were milk cows, laying hens, fruit and pecan orchards, blueberry bushes, and a huge year-round garden that I saw as a pitiless slave master. Before playtime, homework, school events, or anything else came the daily chores. The afternoons of my childhood were spent picking, plunking, peeling, cracking, shelling, husking, and churning. Despite my grumbling, payoff came at the supper table.

Dining was a ritual we were as conditioned to as Pavlov's dog. It started at dusk when my father, in overalls and work boots, came in from the fields. While he scrubbed his hands with brown soap, as diligent as a surgeon, I began setting the table. It was my job to put ice in oversized goblets and pour the tea, sweet as cane syrup and served year-round. We sat down at the table, said grace, and then began passing around the supper dishes.

In the center of the table would be a platter of fried chicken with gravy, fresh pork chops, or country-fried steak. The bowls we passed might hold butterbeans, field peas, creamed corn, stewed squash, fried okra, or sliced tomatoes. The iron skillet was full of cornbread and the napkin-covered basket stacked with biscuits. If strawberries weren't growing in the garden, then it might be peach or blackberry cobbler spooned into dessert dishes and topped with heavy cream. Our food may have changed with the seasons, but one thing didn't change: Everything that graced the table came straight from our fields.

Cassandra King

Author of *Queen of Broken Hearts, The Same Sweet Girls, The Sunday Wife,* and *Making Waves*

From the desk of
CASSANDRA KING
- So many books to write, so little time -
UNITED STATES AIR FORCE
INTERNATIONAL

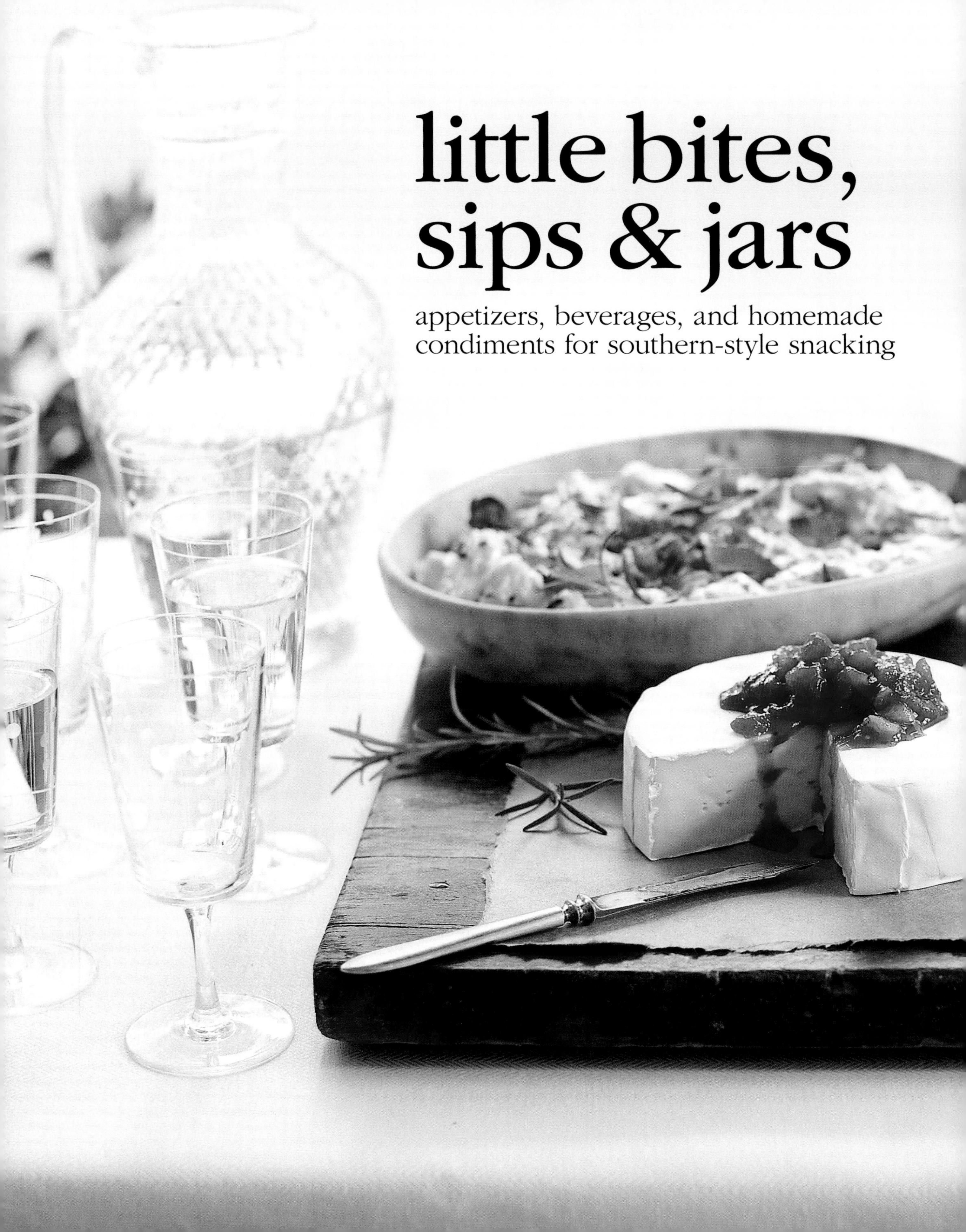

little bites, sips & jars

appetizers, beverages, and homemade condiments for southern-style snacking

brown sugar-bacon wrapped scallops

On my first job interview after culinary school, I was asked to cook scallops. I fell in love with them that very day. Wrapping them in bacon and broiling them is a foolproof way to please any seafood fan.

24 center-cut bacon slices (1½ [12-oz.] packages)
½ cup firmly packed light brown sugar
1 tsp. freshly ground pepper
24 medium-size sea scallops (about 1 lb.)
Wooden picks
Garnish: chopped chives

1. Preheat broiler with oven rack 5 inches from heat. Cook bacon, in 5 batches, in a large skillet over medium-low heat 3 minutes or just until beginning to brown. Remove from heat; drain on paper towels.
2. Combine brown sugar and pepper in a small bowl, stirring until blended. Coat 1 side of each bacon slice with brown sugar mixture. Wrap 1 bacon slice around each scallop, placing sugared side of bacon against widest side of scallop and rolling until bacon ends overlap. Secure bacon with wooden picks.
3. Line a jelly-roll pan with aluminum foil. Place a wire rack in pan. Place scallops on rack.
4. Broil 2 minutes. Turn scallops, and broil 2 more minutes or until bacon is cooked and scallops are plump. Garnish, if desired. Serve immediately.
Makes: 8 to 9 servings Hands-on Time: 30 min. Total Time: 35 min.

chèvre and cucumber stars

Whether you are gathering for bridge, heading to a picnic, or tailgating before a football game, these little stars fit right into the plan. The little scraps left over after cutting the stars make an ideal snack for the lucky cook.

6 oz. goat cheese
4 oz. cream cheese, softened
⅓ cup finely diced Vidalia onion
½ tsp. chopped fresh thyme, plus fresh sprigs for garnish
⅛ tsp. salt
1 English cucumber
1 (16-oz.) package thin white bread slices (such as Pepperidge Farm Very Thin white bread, 28 slices total)

1. Whisk together first 5 ingredients until blended and slightly fluffy.
2. Cut cucumber into 42 (⅛-inch-thick) slices.
3. Spread 1 side of each bread slice with about 1 Tbsp. goat cheese mixture. Top half of bread slices with cucumber slices (3 slices each). Top with remaining bread slices, cheese sides down. Cut sandwiches into stars using a 4-inch star-shaped cutter. Garnish, if desired. Serve 2 to 3 stars per person.
Makes: 14 stars Hands-on Time: 45 min. Total Time: 45 min.

Note: These sandwiches can be made up to 4 hours ahead.

bacon deviled eggs

I've adored deviled eggs for as long as I can remember. We never had a Sunday lunch at my grandmother Tom's without her cut-glass egg platter on the table. Set the kitchen timer for perfectly cooked eggs.

12 large eggs
½ cup mayonnaise
3 cooked bacon slices, crumbled, plus more for garnish
1 Tbsp. chopped fresh parsley
⅛ tsp. salt
⅛ tsp. dry mustard
Pinch of freshly ground pepper

1. Place eggs in a single layer in a stainless-steel saucepan. (Do not use nonstick.) Add water to a depth of 3 inches. Bring to a rolling boil; cover, remove from heat, and let stand 10 minutes. Drain. Submerge eggs in cold water. Tap each egg firmly on the counter until cracks form all over the shell. Peel under cold running water.
2. Slice eggs in half lengthwise; carefully remove yolks, keeping egg white halves intact.
3. Place yolks in a bowl. Mash yolks with mayonnaise until creamy. Stir in bacon and next 4 ingredients. Spoon yolk mixture into egg white halves, using a teaspoon or a small scoop. Garnish, if desired.
Makes: 12 servings   Hands-on Time: 15 min.   Total Time: 30 min.

divine pimiento cheese

If I could choose my last meal, it would have to include pimiento cheese. There are very few days when my fridge isn't home to a batch of the famous spread. I make it often and love it best on soft white sandwich bread. You can also serve it with your favorite crackers.

1 (16-oz.) block sharp Cheddar cheese
¾ cup mayonnaise
1 (4-oz.) jar diced pimiento, drained
2 Tbsp. grated Vidalia onion
Garnish: freshly ground pepper

1. Grate cheese using the large holes of a box grater.
2. Combine cheese and next 3 ingredients, stirring until blended. Store in an airtight container in refrigerator up to 4 days. Garnish, if desired.
Makes: about 3 cups   Hands-on Time: 10 min.   Total Time: 10 min.

fried green tomatoes with red bell pepper sauce

Easy access to green tomatoes is one of the main reasons I dig in the garden each spring. Before tomatoes soften and turn red, they are tart, firm, and gloriously green. These slices are especially good right out of the frying pan.

Vegetable oil
1 cup plain yellow cornmeal
1 cup all-purpose flour
1 tsp. salt
½ tsp. freshly ground pepper
2 large eggs
¼ cup buttermilk
1 lb. green tomatoes (2 large)
Red Bell Pepper Sauce

1. Pour vegetable oil to depth of ¼ inch in a large skillet; heat to 350° over medium-high heat.
2. Meanwhile, combine cornmeal and next 3 ingredients in a large bowl. Combine eggs and buttermilk in a small bowl.
3. Peel tomatoes with a vegetable peeler, and cut into ½-inch-thick slices. Dredge slices in cornmeal mixture, pressing to adhere. Dip in egg mixture, and dredge in cornmeal mixture again, pressing to adhere.
4. Fry tomatoes, in 2 batches, in hot oil 3 minutes on each side or until golden brown. Drain on a wire rack. Serve immediately with Red Bell Pepper Sauce.
Makes: 4 servings Hands-on Time: 30 min.
Total Time: 1 hr., 2 min., including sauce

red bell pepper sauce

3 red bell peppers
1 garlic clove
1 Tbsp. chopped fresh parsley
3 Tbsp. balsamic vinegar
½ tsp. salt
¼ tsp. freshly ground black pepper
¼ cup extra virgin olive oil

1. Preheat oven to 500°. Bake bell peppers on an aluminum foil-lined baking sheet, turning once, 12 to 14 minutes or until peppers look blistered. Place peppers in a large zip-top plastic freezer bag; seal and let stand 10 minutes to loosen skins. Peel peppers; remove and discard seeds. Coarsely chop peppers.
2. Pulse garlic in a food processor until minced. Add chopped pepper, parsley, and next 3 ingredients. Process until mixture is pureed, stopping to scrape down sides as needed. With processor running, pour oil through food chute in a slow, steady stream, processing until smooth.
Makes: 1⅓ cups Hands-on Time: 10 min. Total Time: 32 min.

sweet potato chips with gorgonzola sauce

A homemade potato chip is worlds better than one from a bag. Using a mandoline makes the slicing go faster and ensures that each slice is the same thickness. The hardest part is keeping "tasters" away from the chips before arranging them on the platter.

3 lb. sweet potatoes, peeled
1¼ cups crumbled Gorgonzola cheese, divided
½ cup mayonnaise
5 Tbsp. half-and-half
1 tsp. garlic powder
Vegetable oil
¾ cup chopped green onions

1. Cut potatoes into ⅛-inch-thick slices using a mandoline or knife.
2. Stir together ¼ cup Gorgonzola cheese and next 3 ingredients in a bowl; cover and chill.
3. Pour oil to depth of 2 inches in a large Dutch oven; heat to 375°. Fry potato slices, in batches, 3 minutes or until browned. Drain in a single layer on paper towel-lined wire racks. (The chips will crisp as they drain.)
4. Pile chips on a serving platter. Drizzle with Gorgonzola mixture. Sprinkle with green onions and remaining 1 cup Gorgonzola cheese.
Makes: 10 to 12 servings Hands-on Time: 45 min. Total Time: 45 min.

vidalia spread

I grew up in Vidalia country and enjoy the famous sweet onions in nearly everything. I still get excited to see the first green tops peeping through the sandy soil, a hint of the coming onion season. This ultra-rich dip, served warm, is always a part of my menu when friends visit.

4 bacon slices
2 Vidalia onions, diced (about 4 cups)
1 (8-oz.) package cream cheese, softened
⅓ cup mayonnaise
4 oz. goat cheese
2 Tbsp. all-purpose flour
1½ tsp. chopped fresh rosemary, plus more for garnish
⅛ tsp. salt
Crackers and crudités

1. Preheat oven to 350°. Cook bacon in a large skillet over medium heat 5 minutes or until crisp; remove bacon, and drain on paper towels, reserving 2 tsp. drippings in skillet. Crumble bacon.
2. Sauté onion in hot drippings over medium heat 6 minutes or until translucent. Transfer to a medium bowl. Stir in cream cheese and next 5 ingredients. Spread into an ungreased 8-inch square baking dish.
3. Bake at 350° for 25 minutes. Remove from oven, and top with crumbled bacon. Let stand 5 minutes. Garnish, if desired. Serve warm with crackers and crudités.

Makes: 6 to 8 servings Hands-on Time: 21 min. Total Time: 51 min.

fried pickles with rémoulade dipping sauce

The best Southern flavors collide in fried pickles. They're tangy on the inside, crisp and salty on the outside, and instantly addictive.

Vegetable oil
1 cup all-purpose flour
1 cup plain cornmeal
1 tsp. salt
½ tsp. freshly ground pepper
½ cup beer
1 large egg, lightly beaten
1 (16-oz.) jar dill pickle chips, drained
Rémoulade Dipping Sauce

1. Pour oil to depth of 1 inch into a large skillet; heat to 375°.
2. Combine flour and next 3 ingredients in a shallow bowl.
3. Combine beer and egg in a small bowl. Dredge each pickle in cornmeal mixture; dip in beer mixture, and dredge in cornmeal mixture again.
4. Fry pickles, in 4 batches, 2 minutes or until browned. Drain on wire rack. Serve with Rémoulade Dipping Sauce.

Makes: 8 servings Hands-on Time: 25 min.
Total Time: 35 min., including dipping sauce

rémoulade dipping sauce

1 cup mayonnaise
2 Tbsp. chopped fresh parsley
2 Tbsp. finely chopped onion
1½ Tbsp. tomato paste
1 Tbsp. fresh lemon juice
⅛ tsp. salt
Dash of freshly ground pepper
Hot sauce

1. Combine first 7 ingredients in a small bowl. Add hot sauce to taste.

Makes: 1 cup Hands-on Time: 10 min. Total Time: 10 min.

signature pieces:
milk glass pitchers

Serving pieces made from opaque white glass have been on tables for centuries, but milk glass gained popularity in the late 1800s. Its name comes naturally; the clean white glass is the color of milk. While pitchers are popular, platters, plates, vases, and bowls are among the many tabletop pieces made of milk glass. Plates and platters commonly have crimped or latticed edges.

Milk glass pitchers tend to be thick and fairly heavy. The outside surfaces are often patterned. Hobnail, diamond, or basket-weave are the most common designs. After years of holding sweet tea, milk glass pitchers passed down in the South often come with lightly stained interiors.

summer fruit sangría

If the weather is warm and guests are over, there's a pretty good chance I'll be serving sangría. Using white wine shows off summer's finest fruit. The longer the sangría chills, the fruitier it becomes.

1 (750-milliliter) bottle chilled dry white wine (such as Sauvignon Blanc)
1 (5.5-oz.) can peach nectar
1 peach, sliced
6 strawberries, sliced
12 fresh cherries, pitted and halved

1. Combine wine and peach nectar in a glass pitcher. Add peach slices and next 2 ingredients, and chill 4 to 24 hours before serving.

Makes: 6 cups **Hands-on Time:** 10 min. **Total Time:** 4 hr., 10 min.

blackberry mint julep

Blackberries, mint, and bourbon make this the Triple Crown of juleps. It's a sweet, refreshing cocktail that's powerful yet approachable. The muddled mint and fruit nestle comfortably under the ice for added flavor and color.

- ¼ cup firmly packed fresh mint leaves
- 1 Tbsp. sugar
- 4 large blackberries
- 1 lemon wedge, cut into pieces (remove and discard seeds)
- Finely crushed ice
- ¼ cup (2 oz.) fine Kentucky bourbon
- ¼ cup (2 oz.) seltzer water or club soda
- Garnishes: blackberries, lemon wedge, fresh mint sprig

1. Place mint leaves in a 12-oz. julep cup. Add sugar, blackberries, and lemon wedges. Muddle well to dissolve sugar and release flavors.
2. Fill cup three-fourths full with ice; add bourbon. Stir well with an iced-tea spoon until blended, dispersing all ingredients throughout the drink.
3. Top with seltzer water, and stir. Add more sugar to taste, if desired. Garnish, if desired.

Makes: 1 (12-oz.) serving   Hands-on Time: 5 min.   Total Time: 5 min.

raspberry lemonade

Southern drugstore soda fountains were known for glasses full of fresh lemonade streaked pink by maraschino cherries. For a fresh take on an old favorite, stir up a pitcher of this raspberry version for the kids. To please the "kids at heart," add Champagne.

1½ cups fresh raspberries
1⅓ cups sugar, divided
¼ vanilla bean
1 cup fresh lemon juice (about 7 lemons)
½ cup loosely packed fresh mint leaves
1 lemon, thinly sliced

1. Place raspberries in a large pitcher, and sprinkle with ⅓ cup sugar.
2. Bring remaining 1 cup sugar and 1 cup water to a boil in a small saucepan. Split vanilla bean, scrape seeds into pan, and add bean. Bring to a boil, and boil, stirring occasionally, 3 to 5 minutes or until sugar is dissolved. Remove from heat, cover, and steep 20 minutes.
3. Remove vanilla bean from syrup; discard. Pour syrup over berries in pitcher. Add lemon juice and 1½ qt. water. Stir well, being careful not to crush berries. Cover and chill 1 hour before serving. Stir in mint and lemon slices just before serving. Serve over ice.
Makes: 9 cups Hands-on Time: 10 min. Total Time: 1 hr., 36 min.

sugar sweet tea

I was raised on tea as sweet as dessert. I keep to my heritage and make my tea the same way my grandmother always made hers. As I've gotten older, I've found it a common courtesy to serve decaffeinated tea anytime after lunch.

4 cups water
2 family-size tea bags
¾ cup sugar
4 cups cold water
Lemon wedges

1. Bring 4 cups water to a boil in a saucepan; add tea bags. Boil 1 minute; remove from heat. Cover and steep 5 minutes.
2. Remove and discard tea bags. Add sugar, stirring until dissolved. Pour into a 1-gal. pitcher, and add 4 cups cold water. Serve over ice with lemon wedges.
Makes: 8 cups Hands-on Time: 5 min. Total Time: 15 min.

strawberry-basil jam

5 (8-oz.) canning jars with two-piece lids
2 lb. fresh strawberries
2½ cups sugar
2 Tbsp. fresh lemon juice (about 1 lemon)
2 large fresh basil sprigs
1 (1¾-oz.) package powdered pectin

1. Sterilize jars, and prepare lids as described on page 73.
2. While jars are boiling, wash and hull strawberries. Crush berries in a 6-qt. stainless-steel or enameled Dutch oven or other large, heavy, nonreactive saucepan using a potato masher. Add sugar and next 2 ingredients. Bring to a rolling boil over high heat. Boil, stirring frequently, 10 minutes.
3. Sprinkle pectin over strawberry mixture, and stir well. Return to a rolling boil. Boil 1 minute; remove from heat. Skim foam from surface with a metal spoon; discard. Remove and discard basil sprigs.
4. Fill and process jars as described on page 73. Store properly sealed jars in a cool, dark place. Let stand at least 1 week for the best flavor and texture.
Makes: 5 (8-oz.) jars Hands-on Time: 25 min.
Total Time: 50 min., plus 1 week standing time

spiced tomato refrigerator jam (pictured on page 46)

Sweet and hot spices give summer tomatoes a little kick—and extend their shelf life a few weeks—in this easy refrigerator jam. Enjoy it with Brie and crackers.

4 lb. tomatoes (about 6 large)
1 cup sugar
¼ cup golden raisins
¼ cup fresh lemon juice (about 1 large or 2 medium lemons)
1 Tbsp. balsamic vinegar
1 tsp. dried crushed red pepper
½ tsp. ground cinnamon
¼ tsp. kosher salt
¼ tsp. ground cloves

1. Cut a large "X" in bottom of each tomato. Place tomatoes in a large pot of boiling water; boil 1 to 2 minutes or until peel begins to separate from tomato flesh. Remove with a slotted spoon. Rinse immediately with cold running water, or plunge into ice water to stop the cooking process; drain. Peel back tomato skin using a paring knife or fingers, and discard skin. Cut tomatoes into fourths, core, and squeeze out and discard as many seeds as possible.
2. Dice tomatoes, and put in a 6-qt. stainless-steel or enameled Dutch oven, or other large, heavy, nonreactive saucepan. Stir in sugar and remaining ingredients. Bring to a boil over medium-high heat; reduce heat to medium-low, and simmer, stirring frequently, 30 minutes or until thick and the consistency of jam.
3. Ladle jam into clean canning jars or other heatproof, nonreactive containers with lids. Let cool 10 minutes; cover and chill up to 2 weeks.
Makes: 4 (8-oz.) jars Hands-on Time: 30 min. Total Time: 1 hr., 15 min.

blueberry and lemon preserves

I can't seem to get enough blueberries in the summer. When the season is here, I'm always freezing, canning, cooking, and snacking on those little blue gems. One of my favorite quick eats is a fancy PB&J made with almond butter and these syrupy, lemon-studded preserves.

7 (8-oz.) canning jars with two-piece lids
6 pt. fresh blueberries
4 cups sugar
2 small lemons, quartered and thinly sliced (remove and discard seeds)
3 Tbsp. fresh lemon juice (about 1 large lemon)

1. Sterilize jars, and prepare lids as described on page 73.
2. While jars are boiling, wash blueberries. Combine blueberries and remaining ingredients in a 6-qt. stainless-steel or enameled Dutch oven, or other large, heavy, nonreactive saucepan.
3. Bring to a rolling boil over medium-high heat. Reduce heat to medium-low, and simmer, stirring occasionally, 30 minutes. (A small dab of the syrup mixture spooned onto a cold plate and put in the freezer for 1 minute should thicken to the consistency of honey.)
4. Fill and process jars as described on page 73. If you have any remaining mixture that does not fit in the jars, store it in an airtight container in the refrigerator, and use within a few days. Store properly sealed jars in a cool, dark place. Let stand at least 1 week before serving for the best flavor and texture.
Makes: 7 (8-oz.) jars Hands-on Time: 1 hr., 15 min.
Total Time: 1 hr., 15 min., plus 1 week standing time

Ball
PERFECT
MASON
ATLAS

general canning instructions

To prepare for canning

Use glass jars and two-piece lids specifically designed for home canning. Jars and lid rings can be reused, but you must always use new metal lids, which can be purchased separately. Be sure that the jars, rings, and lids are clean, and that the jars are undamaged and the rims are free of chips or scratches.

Keep the lid rings handy, along with a wide-mouth funnel; a ladle for filling the jars; a thin, plastic utensil for removing air bubbles; a jar lifter; and a clean paper towel. Put a clean, folded towel on the counter near the canning pot, and a second folded towel on the counter in a nearby spot where the processed jars can be set to cool undisturbed.

To sterilize jars and prepare lids

Put clean jars on a rack in a large pot, and cover with water. (You can use a specially designed canning pot or any large stockpot, as long as it has a rack to hold the jars off the bottom of the pot. It should also be deep enough to hold the jars and water to cover by 1 to 2 inches without overflowing when boiling.) Cover the pot, and bring to a full rolling boil. To sterilize the jars, boil 10 minutes;* then reduce the heat, and maintain at a brisk simmer until jars are ready to be filled.

Put the metal lids in a heatproof bowl, making sure they are not stacked tightly together. Just before filling the jars, ladle enough simmering water from the canning pot over the lids to cover them completely, and keep them hot until ready to seal.**

To fill and process jars of fruit preserves, jams, and jellies

Using the jar lifter, remove the jars from the simmering water, and carefully pour all of the water inside them back into the pot. Place the jars upright on the folded towel you set near the pot. Put the funnel in a hot jar, and ladle in the preserves, jam, or jelly, keeping the ladle low and close to the opening of the funnel to prevent excess bubbles from forming inside the jars. Leave ¼-inch headspace at top of each jar. Quickly repeat with the remaining jars.

Remove any air bubbles inside the jars by sliding a thin plastic utensil between the glass and the food and allowing trapped air to escape. Dip the paper towel in hot water, and use it to wipe the jar rims clean. Drain the water from the metal lids back into the canning pot. Quickly place the lids, white sides down, over each jar, and then screw on the lid rings just until finger-tight—do not overtighten.

Use the jar lifter to return the filled jars to the simmering water in the pot, being careful not to tilt the jars and making sure that they are covered with water by 1 to 2 inches. Cover, increase the heat, and return the water to a full rolling boil. Boil 5 minutes.*

Turn off the heat, uncover the pot, and let stand until the boiling has subsided, about 5 minutes. Using the jar lifter, remove the jars from the pot (being sure to keep them upright), and carefully transfer to the second folded towel. Let cool, undisturbed, for 12 to 24 hours.

Check to make sure each fully cooled jar is sealed. If the center of the metal lid cannot be pushed down with your finger, it is sealed. If it depresses and pops up again, the jar is not sealed. It should be refrigerated immediately and its contents used within a few days. Store properly sealed jars in a cool, dry, dark place. They will keep for at least 6 months and up to 1 year.

*Sterilizing and processing times must be adjusted when canning at high altitudes. If you are at 1,001 to 6,000 feet above sea level, add 5 minutes boiling time. If you are at altitudes of 6,001 feet or higher, add 10 minutes boiling time.

**Always check manufacturer's instructions for preparing lids; procedures may vary slightly by brand.

clementine and cranberry chutney

This sunny condiment pairs nicely with roasted chicken, duck, or pork. The key is using small, seedless, easy-to-peel clementines. The pith and membrane of some larger mandarin orange varieties can turn bitter when cooked.

16 small seedless California clementines (such as Cuties; about 2 lb.)
1 cup sugar
⅔ cup sweetened dried cranberries
⅓ cup fresh lime juice (about 5 limes)
¼ cup finely chopped shallots
⅛ tsp. ground allspice

1. Peel clementines, and remove any visible white pith. Separate into segments; cut each segment in half crosswise. Combine clementine pieces and remaining ingredients in a 6-qt. stainless-steel or enameled Dutch oven, or other large, heavy, nonreactive saucepan. Bring to a boil over medium-high heat; boil, stirring often, 10 minutes or until slightly thickened.
2. Transfer to a bowl. Cover and chill until completely cooled (about 2 hours). Store in an airtight container in refrigerator up to 2 weeks.
Makes: 3 cups Hands-on Time: 15 min. Total Time: 2 hr., 30 min.

table talk: sideboard
A sideboard sits near the dining table and gently welcomes guests to the meal. The three to five drawers typically found across the front neatly store serving pieces and linens. Older sideboards have felt-lined drawers, making them ideal for silver and delicate tableware. Some elaborate pieces even have space specifically designed for plates or liquor.

Historically, sideboards were used during mealtimes as buffet tables. In today's home, their usefulness is not limited to the dining room. Designers now use them as storage pieces in entryways, bedrooms, living rooms, bathrooms, and kitchens.

scuppernong jelly

Scuppernongs are a green-gold variety of the sweet and fragrant muscadine grapes that grow in parts of the South. The house I called home until I was an adult had a glorious Scuppernong arbor in the backyard. Picking the thick-skinned, seed-laced grapes became a family affair each September. With a bowl in hand and my feet on a stool, even as a child, I treasured those grapes as much as gold. The sweet but slightly sour aroma that marked the beginning of fall will forever be in my memory.

3 qt. ripe Scuppernong grapes (about 5 lb.)
3 cheesecloth sheets
4 to 6 (8-oz.) canning jars with two-piece lids
2½ to 3¼ cups sugar
2 Tbsp. fresh lemon juice (about 1 lemon)
1 (1¾-oz.) package powdered pectin

1. Wash Scuppernongs; place in a 6-qt. stainless-steel or enameled Dutch oven, or other large, heavy, nonreactive saucepan. Add 1 cup water, and bring to a boil. Boil, stirring frequently, 20 minutes or until most of seeds have been released from pulp, crushing Scuppernongs with a potato masher to slip skins from pulp.
2. Rinse cheesecloth, and wring out excess water. Line a large colander with cheesecloth. Set colander over a large bowl or pot. Pour Scuppernong mixture into cheesecloth, and let stand at least 1 hour. Measure liquid (you should have about 4½ cups), and return to Dutch oven, discarding solids.
3. Sterilize jars, and prepare lids as described on page 73.
4. While jars are boiling, add ¾ cup sugar for each 1 cup juice to Scuppernong juice in Dutch oven. Add lemon juice. Bring to a rolling boil. Boil 5 minutes, stirring frequently.
5. Sprinkle in pectin, stir well, and return to a rolling boil. Boil 1 minute. Remove from heat, and let stand until boiling subsides. Skim foam from surface with a metal spoon, and discard.
6. Fill and process jars as described on page 73. Store properly sealed jars in a cool, dark place. Let stand at least 1 week before serving to allow jelly to fully set. Serve on biscuits or with Brie and crackers, if desired.

Makes: 4 to 6 (8-oz.) jars Hands-on Time: 45 min.
Total Time: 1 hr., 41 min., plus 1 week standing time

fig preserves

I was once the blessed owner of a prolific Brown Turkey fig tree. When the fruit ripened, I competed with the birds and the wasps for every fig possible so I could fill my cupboards with jars of these fig preserves.

3 lb. Brown Turkey figs, stemmed
4 cups sugar
1 small lemon, cut into fourths, seeded, and thinly sliced
¼ cup fresh lemon juice (about 1 large lemon)
Parchment or wax paper
7 (8-oz.) canning jars with two-piece lids

1. Cut figs into quarters, if large, and halves, if small. Layer with sugar and lemon slices in a 6-qt. stainless-steel or enameled Dutch oven, or other large, heavy, nonreactive saucepan. Add lemon juice and 2 cups water. Bring to a boil, without stirring.
2. Remove from heat, and pour mixture into a large bowl or Dutch oven. Let cool 30 minutes. Place a piece of parchment or wax paper directly on mixture, and chill 8 to 12 hours.
3. Return fig mixture to Dutch oven, and bring to a boil. Boil, stirring occasionally, 45 minutes or until figs and lemon slices are translucent and syrup has thickened slightly, skimming and discarding foam from surface as mixture cooks.
4. Meanwhile, sterilize jars, and prepare lids as described on page 73.
5. Fill and process jars as described on page 73. Store properly sealed jars in a cool, dark place. Let stand at least 1 week before serving for the best flavor and texture.
Makes: 7 (8-oz.) jars   Hands-on Time: 35 min.
Total Time: 10 hr., plus 1 week standing time

green tomato chowchow

My version of this popular pickled relish is sweetened with onions and sorghum.

- 2 lb. green tomatoes, cored and chopped (6 cups)
- 1 Vidalia onion, chopped (2 cups)
- ½ cup diced red bell pepper
- ⅓ cup seeded and minced red jalapeño pepper
- 1 Tbsp. kosher salt
- ¾ cup cider vinegar (5% acidity)
- ⅔ cup sugar
- 2 tsp. sorghum syrup
- 1 tsp. dried crushed red pepper
- ½ tsp. celery seeds

1. Pulse tomato and onion, in batches, in a food processor until minced but not pureed. Transfer to a large stainless-steel or enameled Dutch oven, or other heavy, nonreactive saucepan, and stir in bell pepper and next 2 ingredients. Cover and chill 8 to 24 hours.

2. Uncover Dutch oven, and bring tomato mixture to a rolling boil. Pour mixture into a large, fine wire-mesh strainer set over a bowl, and press out as much liquid as possible. Discard liquid; return solids to Dutch oven. Add vinegar and remaining ingredients; bring to a boil. Boil 5 minutes. Ladle into clean canning jars or other heatproof, nonreactive containers with lids. Let cool slightly (about 10 minutes). Cover and chill. Store in refrigerator up to 3 weeks.

Makes: 2 (8-oz.) jars Hands-on Time: 35 min. Total Time: 8 hr., 45 min.

pickled beets with allspice and ginger

I can still see the white bowl with bright maroon pickles that my grandmother placed in the middle of her glass-topped table so every fork could reach. All these years later, I remember her slightly pink fingertips on the days she made pickled beets.

- 6 fresh medium beets (about 3 lb.)
- ½ sweet onion, cut into ¼-inch-thick slices (about 1¼ cups)
- 3 (⅛-inch-thick) fresh ginger slices
- 1 tsp. black peppercorns
- ¾ tsp. whole allspice
- 2 cups cider vinegar (5% acidity)
- ¾ cup sugar
- 2 tsp. kosher salt

1. Trim beet stems to 1 inch; gently wash. Place in a medium saucepan with water to cover. Bring to a boil; cover, reduce heat, and simmer 25 to 30 minutes or until tender. Drain, rinse, and cool slightly (about 15 minutes).

2. Peel beets, halve lengthwise, and cut crosswise into ¼-inch-thick slices.

3. Divide beets and onion slices among clean canning jars or other heatproof, nonreactive containers with lids. Divide ginger and next 2 ingredients among jars.

4. Combine vinegar, remaining ingredients, and 1 cup water in a medium saucepan. Bring to a boil, stirring to dissolve sugar and salt. Pour hot vinegar mixture into jars, covering beet mixture completely and filling to ½ inch from top. Let cool 10 minutes; cover and chill 24 hours before serving. Store in refrigerator up to 3 weeks.

Makes: 3 (1-pt.) jars Hands-on Time: 15 min.
Total Time: 1 hr., 15 min., plus 1 day for chilling

Ball

pickled okra

For canning newcomers, this quick pickle is a great place to start. Designed to keep in the refrigerator and not the pantry, it's easy to make and a fun snack for parties.

1 lb. small fresh okra, stem ends trimmed
2 garlic cloves
2 dried red chile peppers
1 tsp. dried crushed red pepper
1½ cups cider vinegar (5% acidity)
1 cup distilled or filtered water
1½ tsp. kosher salt

1. Bring water to a boil in a saucepan; add okra, and boil 2 minutes or until crisp-tender. Drain. Plunge into ice water to stop the cooking process; drain.
2. Place okra in 2 clean canning jars or other heatproof, nonreactive containers with lids. Divide garlic, chile peppers, and crushed red pepper between jars.
3. Bring vinegar, distilled water, and salt to a boil in a small stainless-steel or other nonreactive saucepan, stirring to dissolve salt. Pour hot vinegar mixture into jars, covering okra mixture completely and filling to ½ inch from tops; discard any remaining vinegar mixture. Let cool 10 minutes. Cover and chill 4 days before serving. Store in refrigerator up to 2 weeks.
Makes: 2 (8-oz.) jars Hands-on Time: 30 min.
Total Time: 40 min., plus 4 days for chilling

Note: Using distilled water in Step 3 helps avoid blue garlic cloves. Minerals in some tap water can make garlic cloves turn blue in refrigerator pickles.

hot pepper jelly

In the South, pepper jelly is a classic that's still in style. You can serve it with roasted chicken or drizzle it over crostini with softened cream cheese.

8 (8-oz.) canning jars with two-piece lids
7 cups sugar
1½ cups cider vinegar (5% acidity)
1 cup diced red bell pepper
¼ cup seeded minced jalapeño pepper (about 2 medium)
1 (3-oz.) package liquid pectin

1. Sterilize jars, and prepare lids as described on page 73.
2. While jars are boiling, combine sugar and next 3 ingredients in a 6-qt. stainless-steel or enameled Dutch oven, or other large, heavy, nonreactive saucepan. Bring to a rolling boil over medium-high heat, stirring frequently. Stir in pectin; return to a rolling boil (about 30 seconds). Boil exactly 1 minute. Remove from heat. Let stand until boiling subsides.
3. Fill and process jars as described on page 73. Let stand at least 1 week to allow jelly to fully set. Store properly sealed jars in a cool, dark place.
Makes: 8 (8-oz.) jars Hands-on Time: 50 min.
Total Time: 50 min., plus 1 week standing time

Note: Peppers will float. Stir to redistribute them when you open a fresh jar.

my southern table

A long time ago at our dining room table, my mother showed me the meaning of hospitality. I grew up in the West End neighborhood of Atlanta, where my family rented a house and took in boarders during the Great Depression. For a dollar a day, a boarder got a bed and two meals. Every morning, long before the sun rose, Mother was in the kitchen making biscuits and cream gravy, frying streak o' lean, and scrambling eggs. Everything is good if you have hot biscuits and cream gravy to go with it.

After school I sometimes worked alongside her in the kitchen shucking corn, shelling peas, setting the table, and washing dirty dishes. I've never known anyone to work harder or longer to please others than my mother, and she received her reward every night: compliments on her cooking from the boarders.

On Saturday night, she would already be preparing for Sunday dinner. She salted and peppered her chicken and left it in the icebox all night before frying it the next day in a big iron skillet with a lid. The lid steamed the chicken as it fried and kept it more moist. (Years later I used the same concepts of marinating and cooking when I developed the Chick-fil-A Chicken Sandwich.) She never used a recipe. She had an instinct, or an intuition, that guided her through everything she cooked, from fried chicken to sweet potato pie.

My mother also had an intuition with people. She wanted every boarder to feel like family and our house to feel like their home. When they came home, she always asked about their day, and she never rushed anyone from the table. With her good food and gentle spirit, Mother made friendships that lasted a lifetime. To me, that was the definition of Southern hospitality.

S. Truett Cathy
Founder and Chairman
Chick-fil-A, Inc.

MOR
CHIKIN
Chick-fil-A
Chick-fil-A
Chick-fil-A
PEPPER

dinner bell

hearty main dishes for satisfying weeknight dinners and Sunday suppers

MAINSTREAM!
SWEETWATER
BREWING COMPANY

lowcountry boil (pictured on pages 86-87)

The best Lowcountry boils involve adding each ingredient at just the right time to ensure everything is perfectly seasoned and nothing is overcooked. When the weather is nice, I like to cook these coastal one-pot meals outside in a turkey fryer, spread some newspapers on a picnic table, and serve right off the paper. Feeding a crowd doesn't get much easier, or better, than this.

1 (3-oz.) package extra-spicy boil-in-bag shrimp-and-crab boil
1 (12-oz.) bottle pale ale beer
1 lemon, cut in half
3 lb. baby red potatoes
2 lb. mild or hot smoked sausage, cut into 2-inch pieces
6 ears fresh corn, cut in half
2 lb. unpeeled, medium-size raw shrimp
2 lb. fresh crawfish
Cocktail sauce, tartar sauce, and hot sauce

1. Combine first 3 ingredients and 5 qt. water in a 12-qt. covered stockpot. Bring to a rolling boil over medium heat. Add potatoes and sausage; cover and cook 10 minutes. Add corn; cover and cook 5 minutes.
2. Add shrimp and crawfish; cover and cook 2 minutes. Remove from heat. Let stand, covered, 10 minutes. Drain. Serve with cocktail sauce, tartar sauce, and hot sauce.

Makes: 8 servings   Hands-on Time: 15 min.   Total Time: 1 hr., 20 min.

coconut fried shrimp with sweet-and-spicy peach sauce (pictured on page 90, bottom)

My son calls these "frilly shrimp" because the coconut curls as it fries. I have a hard time getting a full batch to the table with everyone sneaking a shrimp each time they pass by the stove. You can also turn this supper into a salad: Lay the shrimp atop bowls of mixed greens, and drizzle with the sauce.

1 cup peach preserves
¼ cup fresh lime juice (about 3 limes)
½ tsp. Asian sriracha hot chili sauce
1 lb. unpeeled, large raw shrimp
Vegetable oil
1 cup pale ale beer
1 large egg
1 tsp. salt
½ tsp. freshly ground pepper
2 cups all-purpose flour
1 tsp. sugar
1½ cups sweetened flaked coconut
Lime wedges

1. Combine first 3 ingredients in a small saucepan; cook over medium heat, stirring constantly, 1 minute or until preserves melt. Remove from heat.
2. Peel shrimp, leaving tails on; devein, if desired.
3. Pour vegetable oil to depth of 2 inches in a Dutch oven; heat to 350°.
4. Whisk together beer, next 3 ingredients, and 1 cup flour in a shallow bowl until smooth. Whisk together remaining 1 cup flour and sugar in a second shallow bowl.
5. Dredge shrimp in flour and sugar mixture; dip in beer mixture, shaking off excess. Dredge in flaked coconut.
6. Fry shrimp in hot oil, in batches, 1 to 2 minutes or until golden; drain on a wire rack over paper towels. (Between batches, use a slotted spoon to scoop out and discard any coconut in the oil.) Serve shrimp immediately with sauce and lime wedges.

Makes: 4 servings **Hands-on Time:** 35 min. **Total Time:** 35 min.

signature pieces: platters

In the South, platters are plentiful and used for everything from serving holiday meals to holding mail in the office. Smaller, more versatile platters can be put to countless uses in and out of the dining room, while huge platters are usually destined to showcase the Thanksgiving turkey. Some even feature a series of grooves to collect juices and minimize sloshing when the dish is passed.

Platters aren't reserved for special occasions, however. They are also ideal for the more everyday family-style suppers of the South, since they hold a lot and make it easy for people to help themselves. Be sure to select a platter that's not too heavy to carry when it's piled high with food.

skillet barbecued shrimp (pictured on facing page, top)

New Orleans is home to the kind of barbecued shrimp that doesn't require skewers or charcoal. These shrimp swim in a spicy, buttery sauce that practically yells for big pieces of French bread for dipping.

shrimp

2 lb. unpeeled, medium-size raw shrimp
½ tsp. salt
½ tsp. ground red pepper
¼ tsp. sweet paprika

sauce

½ cup unsalted butter
⅓ cup Worcestershire sauce
2 bay leaves
1 Tbsp. fresh lemon juice
½ tsp. ground red pepper
¼ tsp. sweet paprika
⅛ tsp. onion powder
8 oz. brown ale (such as Lazy Magnolia Southern Pecan Nut Brown Ale)

remaining ingredients

2 Tbsp. extra virgin olive oil
2 garlic cloves, minced
2 Tbsp. unsalted butter
1 lemon, cut into thin slices
French bread

1. Prepare Shrimp: Peel shrimp, leaving tails on; devein, if desired. Place shrimp in a large bowl. Combine salt and next 2 ingredients in a small bowl. Sprinkle salt mixture over shrimp, and toss gently to coat.
2. Prepare Sauce: Combine butter and next 6 ingredients in a saucepan. Bring to a boil over medium-high heat. Reduce heat to medium; simmer 5 minutes. Add beer; simmer 5 minutes. Remove from heat.
3. Heat olive oil in a large skillet over medium heat. Add garlic, and cook 1 minute, stirring constantly. Add shrimp, and cook 3 minutes, stirring often. Carefully add sauce, and cook 1 minute. Remove from heat. Add 2 Tbsp. butter, and gently swirl skillet until butter melts. Add lemon slices. Divide among 4 shallow bowls, remove bay leaves, and serve with French bread.
Makes: 4 servings **Hands-on Time: 20 min.** **Total Time: 35 min.**

atlantic shrimp and grits

I fell in love with shrimp and grits while living in Charleston, South Carolina, where I attended culinary school. On trips back home to Georgia, I'd bring a cooler of fresh shrimp. My grandmother Tom would stand on one side of the stove stirring the grits while I peeled the shrimp on the other side. We were quite a team.

2 lb. unpeeled, large raw shrimp
4 cups chicken broth
1 (12-oz.) can evaporated milk
1 tsp. salt
1 cup uncooked stone-ground grits
2 Tbsp. unsalted butter
3½ oz. prosciutto, chopped
1 jalapeño pepper, seeded and diced
1 cup chopped white onion
2 garlic cloves, minced
⅓ cup dry white wine
1½ cups chopped tomato
½ tsp. chopped fresh thyme, plus sprigs for garnish
½ tsp. lemon zest
½ tsp. salt
¼ tsp. freshly ground black pepper

1. Peel shrimp, leaving tails on; devein, if desired. Cover and chill.
2. Bring broth and next 2 ingredients to a boil over medium heat. Add grits; reduce heat to low. Cook, whisking often, 30 minutes or until creamy and tender. (If grits become too thick, add up to ¼ cup water to thin.) Remove from heat, and keep warm.
3. Melt butter in a large skillet over medium heat. Add prosciutto, and cook 3 minutes or until lightly browned. Add jalapeño and next 2 ingredients. Cook, stirring occasionally, 5 minutes or until onion is tender. Stir in wine. Cook 1 minute, stirring to loosen particles from bottom of skillet.
4. Add chopped tomato, and cook 3 minutes. Add shrimp, thyme, and remaining ingredients. Cover and cook 7 to 8 minutes or just until shrimp turn pink. Top each serving of grits with shrimp mixture, and garnish, if desired.
Makes: 4 servings Hands-on Time: 40 min. Total Time: 1 hr., 25 min.

crispy catfish

Vegetable oil
1 cup all-purpose flour
1 cup milk
2 large eggs
2 cups panko (Japanese breadcrumbs)
4 (6-oz.) catfish fillets
¾ tsp. salt
½ tsp. freshly ground pepper
Lemon wedges

1. Pour oil to depth of 3 inches in a Dutch oven; heat to 375° over medium-high heat.
2. Place flour in a shallow bowl. Combine milk and eggs in another shallow bowl. Place panko in a third shallow bowl. Sprinkle both sides of catfish with salt and pepper. Dredge catfish in flour, dip in egg mixture, and dredge in panko.
3. Fry fillets in hot oil 3 minutes or until breadcrumbs are golden brown and fish flakes with a fork. Drain on a wire rack over paper towels. Serve with lemon wedges.

Makes: 4 servings Hands-on Time: 30 min. Total Time: 30 min.

pecan-crusted flounder

On more occasions than I can remember, Mama, my sister, and I stood, jumpy with anticipation, as my dad spun around on the beach preparing to launch a big cast net into the water. One magical throw brought in a flounder. Two hours later, we ate like kings. As this flounder cooks, the butter browns to make a simple pan sauce worthy of this remarkable fish. Use a large spatula to make turning the fish easier.

2 cups pecan pieces
1 large egg
½ tsp. hot sauce
¾ tsp. salt
4 (6-oz.) flounder fillets
⅛ tsp. freshly ground pepper
5 Tbsp. unsalted butter, divided
1 Tbsp. chopped fresh flat-leaf parsley, plus fresh leaves for garnish
2 Tbsp. fresh lemon juice

1. Process pecans in a food processer until coarsely ground; transfer to a plate.
2. Combine egg, hot sauce, and ½ tsp. salt in a shallow bowl. Sprinkle fish with pepper and remaining ¼ tsp. salt. Dip each fish fillet in egg mixture, shaking off excess. Coat both sides of fish with pecans, pressing to adhere.
3. Melt 2 Tbsp. butter in a 12-inch nonstick skillet over medium heat. Add 2 fish fillets; cook 4 to 5 minutes or until browned. Carefully turn fillets, and cook 2 to 3 more minutes or until bottom is browned and fish flakes with a fork. Transfer fish and any loose pecans to a serving platter. Repeat procedure with 2 Tbsp. butter and remaining fillets.
4. Remove skillet from heat. Add parsley, lemon juice, and remaining 1 Tbsp. butter to skillet. Cook until butter melts, stirring to loosen particles from bottom of skillet. Pour sauce over fish. Garnish, if desired, and serve immediately.

Makes: 4 servings Hands-on Time: 30 min. Total Time: 30 min.

stuffed trout wrapped in bacon

My husband is an avid fly fisherman, and I get to cook what he catches. One fall day, we both lucked out, finding a huge school of rainbow and brown trout.

- 4 (½-lb.) rainbow trout, dressed
- 1 tsp. salt
- ½ tsp. freshly ground pepper
- 2 lemons, halved and thinly sliced
- 25 fresh thyme sprigs
- 8 bacon slices

1. Preheat broiler with oven rack 8 inches from heat. Open trout at belly incision, and lay flat like a book. Sprinkle each fish with salt and pepper. Lay 3 lemon slices and 5 thyme sprigs on 1 side of each fish, and fold opposite side over stuffing. Reserve remaining thyme and lemon slices for garnish.
2. Wrap 2 bacon slices crosswise around each fish, leaving some trout skin exposed between the slices. Secure with wooden picks. Arrange fish on a lightly greased aluminum foil-lined jelly-roll pan.
3. Broil 6 minutes on each side or until bacon is browned and fish flakes with a fork. Remove and discard picks. Garnish with reserved lemon and thyme.
Makes: 4 servings Hands-on Time: 18 min. Total Time: 30 min.

salmon croquettes

We had salmon croquettes with canned salmon about twice a month when I was growing up. My version, with fresh salmon and capers, is a little fancier than Mama's.

- 1¼ lb. salmon fillets (1¼ inch thick)
- 1 Tbsp. extra virgin olive oil
- ¼ tsp. dried dillweed
- ⅛ tsp. salt
- ⅛ tsp. freshly ground pepper
- 1¼ cups fine, dry breadcrumbs
- ⅓ cup diced red onion
- 2 large eggs, lightly beaten
- 1 Tbsp. chopped fresh flat-leaf parsley, plus leaves for garnish
- 1 Tbsp. butter, melted
- ½ tsp. lemon zest
- 2 Tbsp. fresh lemon juice, (about 1 lemon) divided
- 2 Tbsp. drained capers, divided
- ½ cup sour cream
- Vegetable oil
- Garnish: lemon wedges

1. Preheat oven to 375°. Rub salmon with olive oil, and sprinkle with dill, salt, and pepper. Place, skin sides down, on an aluminum foil-lined baking sheet.
2. Bake at 375° for 14 minutes. (Centers of salmon will be slightly rare.) Remove and discard salmon skin. Transfer salmon to a bowl; flake into small pieces using 2 forks. Stir in breadcrumbs, next 5 ingredients, and 1 Tbsp. each lemon juice and capers. Cover and chill 1 hour.
3. Shape salmon mixture into 10 patties (2½ inches wide and about ⅓ cup each). Cover; chill 30 minutes to 3 hours. Combine sour cream and remaining 1 Tbsp. each lemon juice and capers. Cover; chill until ready to serve.
4. Pour oil to depth of 1 inch in a Dutch oven; heat to 325°. Fry patties, in batches, 1 to 1½ minutes on each side or until golden brown. Drain on a wire rack over paper towels. Garnish, if desired, and serve with caper sauce.
Makes: 4 to 6 servings Hands-on Time: 30 min. Total Time: 2 hr., 15 min.

white cheese grits-stuffed poblanos

Take-out chiles rellenos don't hold a candle to my Southern version.

6 large poblano peppers
White Cheese Grits
1 cup all-purpose flour
1 cup plain white cornmeal
½ tsp. salt
¼ tsp. freshly ground pepper
3 large eggs
½ cup milk
Vegetable oil
Southern Ranchero Sauce
Garnish: fresh cilantro leaves

1. Preheat broiler with oven rack 5 inches from heat. Place peppers on an aluminum foil-lined baking sheet. Broil 5 minutes on each side or until peppers look blistered and charred. Place peppers in a zip-top plastic freezer bag; seal and let stand 10 minutes to loosen skins. Peel peppers. Cut a small lengthwise slit in 1 side of each pepper, leaving other side and stem intact; remove and discard seeds and membranes. Spoon grits into a clean zip-top plastic freezer bag. Snip off 1 corner of bag to make a small hole. Pipe grits into peppers. Cover; chill 1 hour.
2. Combine flour and next 3 ingredients in a small bowl. Combine eggs and milk in a separate bowl. Pour vegetable oil to depth of 1 inch in a Dutch oven; heat to 375°.
3. Dredge peppers in flour mixture, dip in egg mixture, and dredge again in flour mixture. Fry peppers, 2 at a time, 2 to 3 minutes or until golden brown. Drain on a wire rack over paper towels. Serve with Southern Ranchero Sauce. Garnish, if desired.
Makes: 6 servings   Hands-on Time: 30 min.
Total Time: 2 hr., 50 min., including grits and sauce

white cheese grits

2½ cups chicken broth
⅓ cup uncooked quick-cooking grits
8 oz. Monterey Jack cheese

1. Bring chicken broth to a boil in a saucepan over medium-high heat. Add grits; simmer, stirring often, 25 minutes.
2. Grate cheese on the large holes of a box grater. Remove grits from heat, and stir in cheese. Let cool until just warm to the touch.
Makes: 2 cups   Hands-on Time: 35 min.   Total Time: 35 min.

southern ranchero sauce

1 cup diced onion
2 garlic cloves, minced
2 Tbsp. seeded and minced jalapeño pepper
1 Tbsp. vegetable oil
1½ cups chopped plum tomatoes
2 Tbsp. chopped fresh cilantro
3 Tbsp. fresh lime juice
½ tsp. salt

1. Cook onion, garlic, and jalapeño in hot oil in a large skillet over medium-low heat 8 minutes or until onion is soft and just beginning to brown. Stir in tomatoes and remaining ingredients. Cook 8 minutes or until slightly thickened.
Makes: 1½ cups   Hands-on Time: 30 min.   Total Time: 30 min.

roasted cornish hens with lemons and creamy grits

These small, tender chickens add elegance to a special occasion.

1½ cups orange juice
¾ cup salt
4 (1½-lb.) Cornish hens
4 lemons, halved, plus more for garnish
4 fresh rosemary sprigs, plus more for garnish
Kitchen string
¼ cup extra virgin olive oil, divided
1¼ tsp. freshly ground pepper, divided
Creamy Grits
1 Tbsp. unsalted butter
1 garlic clove, minced
⅔ cup chicken broth
⅓ cup dry white wine
¼ tsp. salt
Garnish: green olives

1. Whisk together orange juice, ¾ cup salt, and 12 cups water in a large bowl until salt dissolves. Divide between 2 large zip-top plastic freezer bags. Add 2 Cornish hens to each bag. Seal and chill 8 to 24 hours.
2. Preheat oven to 450°. Remove hens from brine, discarding brine. Rinse and pat dry. Stuff 1 lemon half and 1 rosemary sprig in cavity of each hen. Tie legs of hens together with kitchen string. Tuck wing tips under. Rub skin with 2 Tbsp. olive oil. Sprinkle with 1 tsp. pepper. Place on a lightly greased rack in a roasting pan.
3. Rub remaining 4 lemon halves with remaining 2 Tbsp. olive oil. Place lemons on a small pan lined with aluminum foil.
4. Roast hens and lemons at 450° for 45 to 50 minutes or until hens are well browned, juices are clear, and a meat thermometer inserted in thigh registers 165°.
5. Meanwhile, prepare Creamy Grits; keep warm.
6. Remove hens and lemons from oven. Reserve 1 Tbsp. drippings from pan with hens. Cover hens loosely with foil.
7. Heat reserved 1 Tbsp. drippings with butter in a large skillet over medium heat. Add garlic, and cook, stirring constantly, 1 minute or until browned. Add broth and wine, and cook 5 minutes or until reduced by half. Stir in ¼ tsp. salt and remaining ¼ tsp. pepper. Serve hens with Creamy Grits, roasted lemons, and white wine sauce. Garnish, if desired.

Makes: 4 servings   Hands-on Time: 50 min.
Total Time: 9 hr., 35 min., including grits

creamy grits (pictured on cover)

2 cups milk
2 cups chicken broth
½ tsp. salt
1 cup uncooked quick-cooking grits
2 Tbsp. unsalted butter

1. Bring first 3 ingredients to a simmer over medium heat in a saucepan; reduce heat to low. Add grits, and cook, stirring often, 8 minutes or until thickened. Stir in butter.

Makes: 4 cups   Hands-on Time: 15 min.   Total Time: 25 min.

chicken bog

Creamy and comforting, this Lowcountry classic just may be the official chicken soup of the South. I like to eat it with something salty, such as pickled okra or green olives. Some like lemon wedges and hot sauce. Any way—even, and perhaps especially, just plain—it's good for the soul.

1 (4-lb.) whole chicken
4 celery ribs, cut into ½-inch pieces
2 medium-size yellow onions, chopped
3 carrots, cut into ½-inch pieces
5 garlic cloves, smashed
10 fresh parsley sprigs
3 fresh thyme sprigs
2 bay leaves
1 tsp. celery seeds
½ tsp. black peppercorns
1½ cups uncooked extra-long-grain rice (such as Mahatma Gold)
2 tsp. salt
¼ tsp. freshly ground pepper
3 Tbsp. unsalted butter
3 Tbsp. finely chopped fresh parsley
4 sliced green onions, divided
Garnish: sliced pickled okra or green olives

1. Remove giblets and neck, if included, from chicken, and reserve for another use. Place chicken, breast side up, and next 9 ingredients in a large Dutch oven. Add 10 cups water.
2. Bring to a boil over high heat; cover, reduce heat to low, and simmer 1 hour or until chicken is done. Remove chicken from liquid, reserving liquid, and cool slightly (15 minutes).
3. Bring reserved liquid to a boil, and simmer, uncovered, 30 minutes.
4. Meanwhile, remove meat from chicken, and shred into large chunks using a fork. Discard skin and bones.
5. Pour liquid through a wire-mesh strainer into a bowl; discard solids. Skim fat from surface of liquid, or use a fat separator to remove fat.
6. Wipe Dutch oven clean. Place chicken in Dutch oven. Add rice, salt, pepper, and 6 cups strained liquid. (Reserve any remaining liquid for another use.) Bring to a boil over medium heat; cover, reduce heat to low, and cook 25 minutes or until rice is tender and liquid is absorbed. (The bog should still be moist.)
7. Stir in butter. Remove from heat, and stir in parsley and half of green onions. Sprinkle with remaining green onions. Garnish, if desired. Serve warm.
Makes: 6 to 8 servings Hands-on Time: 30 min.
Total Time: 2 hr., 45 min.

real buttermilk fried chicken

To this day, fried chicken is my go-to lunch after church on Sundays. Keeping the shortening hot enough is the key to crisp chicken. Use a thermometer the first few times. After that, judging the heat becomes second nature.

1 (3½-lb.) whole chicken, cut into 8 pieces
2 cups buttermilk
1 Tbsp. Creole seasoning
1 tsp. salt
¼ tsp. freshly ground pepper
3 cups all-purpose flour
9 cups shortening
Garnishes: lemon wedges, fresh flat-leaf parsley

1. Place chicken in a large zip-top plastic freezer bag. Add buttermilk; seal and chill 2 hours.
2. Remove chicken from buttermilk, discarding buttermilk. Sprinkle chicken with Creole seasoning and next 2 ingredients. Place flour on a large plate or in a shallow dish. Dredge chicken in flour, shaking off excess.
3. Melt shortening to depth of 1½ inches in a Dutch oven or heavy-bottomed skillet at least 10 inches wide and 3 inches deep over medium-high heat; heat to 360°. Fry chicken, in batches, turning often, 15 to 20 minutes or until evenly browned and done. Drain on a wire rack over paper towels. Garnish, if desired.

Makes: 6 to 8 servings   Hands-on Time: 50 min.
Total Time: 2 hr., 50 min.

table talk:
banquet table

Since Colonial times, dinner parties have been synonymous with the South. When Congress was in session, Thomas Jefferson hosted a dinner party each night. When it comes to seating a crowd, not much has changed. The longer the guest list, the longer the table needs to be.

Banquet tables that accommodate at least twelve for dinner often have three sections. The middle section is a drop-leaf table that can be removed and used elsewhere in the home on non-banquet days. Without it, the two end sections join together to form a small dining table. When the drop-leaf table is added and fully extended, the seating capacity more than doubles.

white barbecued chicken

White barbecue sauce calls northern Alabama home. Being a Georgia girl, I only learned about it when I lived in Birmingham years ago. I now take this tangy chicken on beach trips when I can let it marinate in the cooler on the long ride down and grill it for supper when we arrive. It's become a family tradition.

2 cups mayonnaise
¾ cup cider vinegar
1½ Tbsp. cracked black pepper
1 Tbsp. light brown sugar
2 Tbsp. fresh lemon juice
½ tsp. ground red pepper
1 (4¼-lb.) cut-up whole chicken
Garnish: rosemary sprigs

1. Combine first 6 ingredients. Set aside 1½ cups; cover and chill remaining sauce.
2. Remove and discard excess fat from chicken. Place chicken in a large zip-top plastic freezer bag. Pour reserved 1½ cups sauce over chicken. Seal bag, and rub to coat chicken. Chill 8 hours.
3. Light one side of grill, heating to 350° to 400° (medium-high) heat; leave other side unlit.
4. Remove chicken from marinade, discarding marinade. Place chicken on lit side of grill, and grill, covered with grill lid, 7 to 10 minutes on each side or until browned and beginning to char. Transfer chicken to unlit side of grill, and grill, covered with grill lid, 25 to 30 minutes or until done. Let stand 5 minutes before serving. Serve with reserved sauce. Garnish, if desired.
Makes: 4 servings Hands-on Time: 35 min. Total Time: 9 hr., 5 min.

cornmeal-crusted chicken livers

Like many Southerners, my husband grew up eating chicken livers, so I like to cook them for him. For the freshest taste, buy livers no more than a day before cooking. It's common for livers to pop and splatter while frying. To minimize mess, use a very deep pot and a splatter screen.

1 lb. chicken livers, drained and tough membranes removed
½ cup Marsala
1 cup plain yellow cornmeal
½ tsp. salt
¼ tsp. freshly ground pepper
3 Tbsp. bacon drippings
3 Tbsp. vegetable oil

1. Combine livers and Marsala in a medium bowl; cover and chill 20 minutes. Drain; discard Marsala. Place cornmeal in a shallow bowl. Sprinkle livers with salt and pepper. Dredge in cornmeal.
2. Heat bacon drippings and oil in a deep, heavy-bottomed Dutch oven over medium heat. Cook livers, in 2 batches turning occasionally, 3 to 4 minutes or until golden brown. Drain on paper towels. Serve immediately.
Makes: 4 servings Hands-on Time: 20 min. Total Time: 40 min.

fried chicken-and-avocado salad

Here's a salad that's hearty and satisfying enough to be a main course any night of the week. I love the textural contrast of crispy chicken and creamy avocados.

4 skinned and boned chicken breasts (about 1¾ lb.)
1 cup buttermilk
2 cups all-purpose flour
2 tsp. salt
¾ tsp. freshly ground pepper
Vegetable oil
3 romaine lettuce hearts, chopped (10 cups)
3 avocados, sliced
1 medium tomato, chopped
1 small red onion, thinly sliced
Jalapeño Dressing
Garnish: chopped fresh cilantro leaves

1. Cut each chicken breast lengthwise into 3 long strips. Combine chicken strips and buttermilk; soak 15 minutes.
2. Combine flour and next 2 ingredients on a plate or in a shallow bowl. Drain chicken, reserving buttermilk. Dredge chicken in flour mixture, shaking to remove excess; dip in buttermilk, and dredge in flour mixture again.
3. Pour oil to depth of 2 inches in a Dutch oven; heat to 350°. Fry chicken, in batches, 5 to 6 minutes or until golden and done. Drain on a wire rack over paper towels.
4. Divide lettuce among 6 plates. Top each with chicken strips, avocado, tomato, and onion. Drizzle with Jalapeño Dressing. Garnish, if desired.
Makes: 6 servings Hands-on Time: 40 min.
Total Time: 1 hr., including dressing

jalapeño dressing

½ cup white balsamic vinegar
¼ cup pickled jalapeño pepper slices
1 tsp. salt
⅔ cup olive oil
½ cup loosely packed fresh cilantro leaves

1. Process first 3 ingredients in a food processor or blender until smooth. With processor running, pour oil through food chute in a slow, steady stream, processing until smooth. Add cilantro, and pulse until blended. Cover and chill until ready to use. Stir or shake before serving.
Makes: 1¼ cups Hands-on Time: 5 min. Total Time: 5 min.

bacon-covered roasted turkey

This recipe gives you triple insurance against the dreaded dry bird: You brine the turkey, rub butter under and over its skin, and lay bacon on top. Choose a fresh turkey—and read the label to make sure it hasn't been injected with a saline or flavor solution—to ensure a juicy and perfectly seasoned holiday centerpiece.

- 2 cups medium-flake kosher salt (such as Diamond Crystal)
- 2 cups firmly packed light brown sugar
- 3 Tbsp. black peppercorns
- 1 Tbsp. mustard seeds
- 1 (12-lb.) whole fresh turkey
- 1 cup unsalted butter, softened
- 2 Tbsp. chopped fresh parsley
- 1 Tbsp. chopped fresh sage
- ½ tsp. table salt
- ½ tsp. freshly ground pepper
- Kitchen string
- 6 bacon slices (not thick cut)
- Garnishes: roasted carrots, fresh bay leaves

1. Combine first 4 ingredients and 2 qt. water in a saucepan, and cook over medium heat 5 minutes or until salt and sugar are dissolved. Remove from heat. Divide liquid between 2 large (10- to 12-cup) bowls; add 4 cups ice cubes to each bowl and enough cold water to make 10 cups of brine in each bowl. Stir until ice melts and both mixtures are completely cool (about 5 minutes).

2. Remove giblets and neck from turkey, and reserve for another use, if desired. Place turkey in an 18-qt. food-grade plastic container or stockpot. Pour brine into cavity and over turkey, covering turkey completely. Place in refrigerator. Cover and chill 24 hours, turning turkey once halfway through.

3. Combine butter and next 4 ingredients in a small bowl.

4. Preheat oven to 350°. Remove turkey from brine, discarding brine. Rinse turkey well, including cavity.

5. Starting at neck, carefully loosen and lift skin from breast and drumsticks using your fingers. (Do not totally detach skin.) Rub ¾ cup butter mixture under skin; carefully replace skin. Tie ends of legs together with string; tuck wing tips under. Place turkey, breast side up, on a lightly greased rack in a roasting pan; rub remaining butter mixture over skin.

6. Roast turkey at 350° for 1 hour and 45 minutes, basting with pan juices every 20 minutes during last 45 minutes of cooking. Remove from oven, and lay bacon slices, crosswise, over breast and drumsticks.

7. Return turkey to oven; roast 45 minutes to 1 hour or until a meat thermometer inserted in thickest portion of thigh registers 170°, basting every 15 minutes. Let stand 30 minutes before carving. Garnish, if desired.

Makes: 8 servings **Hands-on Time:** 50 min.
Total Time: 4 hr., plus 1 day for brining

butter-fried pork chops with nutmeg

Pork chops are one of my dad's specialties. I'm especially fond of these, which are marinated to stay moist, breaded for crunch, and then cooked in butter. Clarifying the butter first ensures that it won't smoke and burn while the chops cook to perfection.

- 2 cups apple juice
- ¼ cup kosher salt
- 4 (¾-inch-thick) center-cut bone-in pork chops (about ½ lb.)
- 6 Tbsp. unsalted butter
- 3 large eggs, lightly beaten
- ½ tsp. ground nutmeg
- 1½ cups fine, dry breadcrumbs
- ⅛ tsp. freshly ground pepper
- Garnishes: lemon slices, parsley

1. Combine juice, salt, and 2 cups water in a large zip-top plastic freezer bag. Seal bag, and shake until salt is dissolved. Add pork. Seal and chill 2 hours.
2. To clarify butter, melt butter in a saucepan over medium-low heat. Skim milk solids (foam) from top of melted butter, and save for another use. Pour melted, clarified butter into a bowl, leaving any remaining solids in pan.
3. Remove pork from marinade, discarding marinade. Pat pork very dry. Combine eggs and nutmeg in a bowl. Combine breadcrumbs and pepper in another bowl. Dip pork in egg mixture, and dredge in breadcrumb mixture.
4. Place half of clarified butter in a large cast-iron skillet over medium-low heat; add 2 pork chops, and cook 4 minutes on each side or until well browned and a meat thermometer inserted into thickest portion registers 145°. Remove from skillet; let stand 3 minutes. Repeat procedure with remaining clarified butter and pork chops. Garnish, if desired.
Makes: 4 servings   Hands-on Time: 35 min.   Total Time: 2 hr., 35 min.

peach-glazed duck breasts

- 4 (6-oz.) boned duck breasts
- ½ cup rice wine vinegar
- ¼ cup extra virgin olive oil
- ½ tsp. salt
- ¼ tsp. freshly ground pepper
- 2 cups sliced fresh peaches (skins removed) or thawed frozen peach slices
- ¼ cup honey
- 2 Tbsp. soy sauce
- 1 Tbsp. rice wine vinegar

1. Make 4 cuts in fat on each duck breast using a paring knife. (Cut through skin and fat only, not meat.) Combine rice wine vinegar and next 3 ingredients in a large zip-top plastic freezer bag. Add duck. Seal and chill 1 hour.
2. Combine peaches and next 3 ingredients in a small saucepan. Bring to a boil over medium heat; reduce heat to medium-low, and simmer 10 minutes.
3. Remove duck from marinade, discarding marinade. Pat duck dry with paper towels. Cook duck, fat side down, in a large skillet over medium heat 6 minutes. Turn and cook 5 minutes (for medium) or to desired degree of doneness. (The fat should be very browned and crispy when turned.) Remove and let stand 5 minutes. Slice duck; spoon peach glaze over duck just before serving.
Makes: 4 servings   Hands-on Time: 30 min.   Total Time: 1 hr., 38 min.

pecan, bourbon, and cane syrup ham

Cured hams retain a rosy color after you cook them. With a fresh, uncured ham like the one here, the meat has a much lighter color after cooking, more like that of pork loin. Fresh hams are usually available in grocery stores around the holidays, but you might have to order them at other times of the year. I like to make this ham before a big holiday, so I can easily feed a crowd for days. I make a meal of it right out of the oven and slice up the rest for later in the week. The butt portion is the rounder side of the ham, with less bone, so it's easier to slice.

1 (10- to 11-lb.) fresh bone-in ham (butt portion)
1 Tbsp. rubbed sage
3 Tbsp. extra virgin olive oil
5 garlic cloves, minced
1 tsp. salt
1 tsp. freshly ground pepper
½ cup cane syrup
¼ cup firmly packed light brown sugar
¼ cup bourbon
1 Tbsp. Dijon mustard
¾ cup chopped pecans
Garnish: Satsuma orange wedges

1. Preheat oven to 325°. Score ham skin and fat, making shallow (⅛-inch-deep) cuts about 1½ inches apart in a diamond pattern.
2. Combine sage and next 4 ingredients. Rub mixture over ham. Place ham, fat side up, on a lightly greased rack in an aluminum foil-lined roasting pan.
3. Bake at 325° for 3 hours. Meanwhile, bring cane syrup and next 3 ingredients to a boil in a medium saucepan over medium-high heat; reduce heat to low, and simmer 3 minutes. Add pecans, and simmer, stirring frequently, 3 minutes or until thick and syrupy.
4. Remove ham from oven. Spread glaze over top of ham. Bake 30 minutes, basting with pan juices every 10 minutes. Shield with foil to prevent excessive browning, and bake 30 more minutes or until a meat thermometer inserted into center of ham registers 145°. Let stand 30 minutes before slicing. Garnish, if desired.
Makes: 16 servings   Hands-on Time: 30 min.   Total Time: 5 hr.

peppered pork roast with blue cheese grits

When it's not cut into chops, the center-cut pork loin makes a mighty bone-in roast and serves a crowd. Make it for company and save some for sandwiches the next day.

5 large garlic cloves
1 (4.5-lb.) bone-in, center-cut pork loin roast, trimmed
1 Tbsp. all-purpose flour
1 Tbsp. whole grain mustard
1 Tbsp. dried parsley flakes
1½ tsp. coarsely ground pepper
¾ tsp. dried thyme
½ tsp. salt
Blue Cheese Grits
Garnish: arugula

1. Preheat oven to 325°. Cut garlic into slivers. Cut ½-inch-deep slits in pork using a paring knife; insert garlic into slits. Place roast, fat side up, on a lightly greased rack in a roasting pan. Pat dry. Sprinkle top of roast with flour; pat lightly to adhere. Spread mustard over roast.
2. Combine parsley and next 3 ingredients. Generously coat roast with parsley mixture, patting to adhere.
3. Bake, uncovered, at 325° for 2 hours and 10 minutes or until a meat thermometer inserted into thickest portion registers 145°. Let stand 5 to 10 minutes before slicing. Serve with Blue Cheese Grits. Garnish, if desired.
Makes: 10 to 12 servings Hands-on Time: 15 min.
Total Time: 3 hr., 20 min., including grits

blue cheese grits

8 cups chicken broth
1 tsp. salt
2 cups uncooked stone-ground grits
5 oz. soft-ripened blue cheese, rind removed (such as Saga Classic Soft-Ripened Blue-Veined Cheese)
2 Tbsp. unsalted butter

1. Bring broth and salt to a boil in a large saucepan over high heat. Stir in grits. Reduce heat, and simmer, stirring very often, 45 minutes or until smooth and creamy.
2. Reserve about one-fifth of the cheese. Slice the rest, and add, with butter, to the grits. Stir until both are melted. Just before serving, garnish with crumbles of the reserved cheese.
Makes: 12 servings Hands-on Time: 50 min. Total Time: 50 min.

spiced and smoked boston butt

Every warm weather holiday when I was growing up, Dad was up before the sun to start the smoker, and the backyard was filled with an aroma that had us all counting down until lunchtime. Vinegar-based sauces, like this Carolina-style sauce, are my favorite way to dress barbecue. Pickles, chow-chow, and buns are optional.

- 1 cup firmly packed light brown sugar
- 3 Tbsp. paprika
- 1 Tbsp. salt
- 1 Tbsp. celery seeds, crushed
- 2 tsp. chili powder
- 1 tsp. garlic powder
- 1 tsp. ground red pepper
- 1 tsp. freshly ground black pepper
- ¾ tsp. ground allspice
- 1 (5-lb.) bone-in pork shoulder roast (Boston butt)
- 10 cups hickory chips
- 1 disposable, aluminum-foil roasting pan
- Vinegar Sauce

1. Combine first 9 ingredients in a small bowl. Place pork in a large bowl. Generously coat all sides with ¾ cup spice rub. Reserve remaining rub for another use. Cover pork with plastic wrap; chill 8 to 24 hours.
2. Soak wood chips in water to cover 30 minutes to 2 hours.
3. Place aluminum-foil pan half-full of water on 1 side of a ceramic smoker (such as a Big Green Egg), under the grate, to collect drippings and keep them from burning. Light hardwood charcoal on the other side of the smoker, and bring internal temperature to 300°. Maintain temperature for 15 to 20 minutes.
4. Drain wood chips, and place 2 cups directly on coals. Place pork, fat side up, on cooking grate over the water pan; cover with smoker lid.
5. Smoke pork, maintaining smoker temperature at 300°, for 6 hours and 30 minutes or until a meat thermometer inserted into thickest portion registers 190° and the meat falls off the bone. Check smoker every 30 minutes, adding wood chips (1 cup at a time) as needed to maintain smoke, and adjusting vents and adding charcoal (5 to 6 pieces at a time) as needed to maintain 300° heat. Keep the lid closed as much as possible. Cover meat with foil when the crust is browned to your liking.
6. Let stand 30 minutes before chopping or pulling. Serve with Vinegar Sauce.
Makes: 8 to 10 servings Hands-on Time: 40 min.
Total Time: 15 hr., 50 min., including sauce

vinegar sauce

- 1½ cups cider vinegar
- 1 cup ketchup
- ⅓ cup firmly packed light brown sugar
- 1 Tbsp. fresh lemon juice
- ¾ tsp. dried crushed red pepper
- ¼ tsp. salt
- ⅛ tsp. freshly ground black pepper

1. Combine all ingredients in a large saucepan. Cook over medium-low heat, stirring occasionally, 5 minutes or until brown sugar dissolves. (Do not boil.) Store in refrigerator up to 3 months.
Makes: 3 cups Hands-on Time: 10 min. Total Time: 10 min.

stuffed meatloaf

This hearty meatloaf is laced with caramelized onions and gooey mozzarella cheese. Lean ground beef labeled 93/7 works best in this recipe, helping the loaf hold together for slicing. If you have any slices left over, save them for Open-Faced Meatloaf Sandwiches *(recipe on page 196).*

2 Tbsp. extra virgin olive oil
1 small white onion, diced
1 small red onion, diced
2¼ lb. lean ground beef
1½ cups soft, fresh breadcrumbs
2 large eggs
½ cup ketchup
1 Tbsp. Worcestershire sauce
¾ tsp. salt
½ tsp. freshly ground pepper
3 oz. fresh mozzarella, cut into ¼-inch-thick slices
Garnishes: ketchup, fresh flat-leaf parsley leaves

1. Preheat oven to 400°. Heat olive oil in a medium skillet over medium-high heat. Add onions, reduce heat to low, and cook, stirring occasionally, 20 to 25 minutes or until onions are caramel colored. Remove from heat, and cool to room temperature (about 20 minutes).
2. Stir together beef and next 6 ingredients in a large bowl. Divide beef mixture into 2 equal portions, and pat each into a 9- x 5-inch oval on a sheet of aluminum foil. Arrange onions on top of 1 oval, leaving a ½-inch border around edges. Top onions with mozzarella slices, leaving a ½-inch border. Use foil to invert remaining oval on top of the mozzarella, remove top foil, and press meat edges to seal. Invert stuffed loaf onto a lightly greased wire rack in an aluminum foil-lined broiler pan (or jelly-roll pan); remove foil used to invert loaf.
3. Bake at 400° for 1 hour or until center is no longer pink. Let stand 15 to 20 minutes before serving. Garnish, if desired.
Makes: 6 servings Hands-on Time: 40 min. Total Time: 2 hr., 15 min.

crispy country-fried steak

Country-fried steak can be fancied up with either white or brown gravy, depending on where in the South it's served. Some like to smother the steak entirely, but I like spooning a little peppery onion gravy on top and serving the rest on the side.

1 cup all-purpose flour
1 tsp. salt
1 tsp. freshly ground pepper
1 tsp. paprika
2 large eggs
2 Tbsp. water
4 (6-oz.) cubed steaks (about 1½ lb.)
½ cup vegetable oil
1 medium-size white or yellow onion, cut into ⅓-inch-thick rings
½ tsp. salt
½ tsp. freshly ground pepper
2 Tbsp. all-purpose flour
1½ cups warm water

1. Combine first 4 ingredients in a large shallow bowl. Whisk together eggs and 2 Tbsp. water in a shallow bowl. Dredge steaks in flour mixture, dip in egg mixture, and dredge again in flour mixture, turning and patting steaks with hands to coat evenly and generously.
2. Cook steaks, in 2 batches, in hot oil in a large cast-iron skillet over medium-high heat 4 minutes on each side or until crisp and golden brown. Drain on paper towels, reserving 2 Tbsp. drippings in skillet.
3. Reduce heat to medium. Add onion, salt, and pepper, and cook 3 minutes or until softened. Stir in 2 Tbsp. flour, stirring to loosen particles from bottom of skillet. Cook, whisking constantly, 4 minutes or until flour is a dark mahogany color. (The pan drippings will already be brown.)
4. Slowly whisk in warm water; bring to a boil, stirring constantly. Reduce heat to medium-low, and simmer 4 minutes or until gravy begins to thicken. Cover, reduce heat to low, and simmer, stirring often, 9 minutes or until gravy is thickened and onions are tender. (If gravy becomes too thick, add water, 1 Tbsp. at a time, to desired consistency.) Season with more salt and pepper, if desired.
5. Arrange steaks on a serving platter. Drizzle with gravy, and top with some of the onions. Serve remaining onions and gravy on the side.
Makes: 4 servings   Hands-on Time: 50 min.   Total Time: 55 min.

oven pot roast with baby vegetables

(pictured on page 123, right)

Meeting at the table over a comforting pot roast is the perfect end to a long winter day. The goal here is fall-apart beef roast and melt-in-your-mouth vegetables. The flavorful liquid in the pot serves as a light, enticing sauce.

1 Tbsp. salt
2 tsp. freshly ground pepper
2 tsp. dried basil
1 tsp. garlic powder
½ tsp. dry mustard
2 (2.5-lb.) boneless chuck roasts, trimmed
¼ cup vegetable oil, divided
3 cups chicken broth
2 cups dry red wine
2⅓ cups pearl onions
1 (8-oz.) package baby portobello mushrooms
1 lb. small (1½-inch) Yukon gold potatoes
8 oz. small carrots with tops or baby carrots
Garnish: fresh bay leaves

1. Preheat oven to 375°. Combine first 5 ingredients in a small bowl. Rub roasts with salt mixture. Heat half of oil in a heavy, ovenproof 5-qt. Dutch oven over medium heat. Cook 1 roast 7 minutes on each side or until well browned. Transfer roast to a jelly-roll pan. Repeat procedure with remaining oil and roast.
2. Remove Dutch oven from heat, and carefully add chicken broth and wine, stirring to loosen particles from bottom of Dutch oven. Bring to a simmer; cook 5 minutes. Return roasts to Dutch oven; cover. (They will be nestled very closely and may overlap slightly.) Bake, covered, at 375° for 2 hours.
3. Bring a small saucepan of water to a boil. Add onions, and cook 1 minute. Drain and peel onions. Cut any large mushrooms in half. Add onions, mushrooms, potatoes, and carrots to Dutch oven with roasts. Bake, covered, 45 minutes. Uncover and bake 15 more minutes or until vegetables are tender. Slice or pull apart roasts, and serve with vegetables and sauce. Garnish, if desired.

Makes: 8 servings Hands-on Time: 35 min. Total Time: 3 hr., 45 min.

coffee-crusted standing rib roast

Deeply roasted, finely ground coffee gives this standing rib roast a dramatically charred crust and intense flavor. For the best taste and finest grind, buy freshly roasted whole beans, and use the grinder at your grocery store or coffee shop. You can also purchase espresso powder that is already finely ground. The coarsest part of this rub will be the cracked pepper.

1 (5-lb.) 2-rib prime rib roast
3 Tbsp. very finely ground dark roast coffee or espresso
2 tsp. kosher salt
2 tsp. cracked pepper
1 tsp. light brown sugar
½ tsp. ancho chile powder
Garnishes: fresh oregano sprigs, horseradish

1. Place roast, rib side down, in a roasting pan. Stir together coffee and next 4 ingredients in a small bowl. Rub coffee mixture over roast. Let stand at room temperature 30 minutes.
2. Arrange oven rack in lower third of oven. Preheat oven to 500°.
3. Bake at 500° for 30 minutes. Reduce heat to 300°, and bake until a meat thermometer inserted in thickest portion registers 135° (medium rare), about 1 hour and 5 minutes. Let stand 20 minutes before serving. Garnish, if desired.
Makes: 4 servings Hands-on Time: 10 min. Total Time: 2 hr., 35 min.

my southern table

For as long as I can remember, the table was the gathering place for my family. I helped out in the kitchen when I was only as tall as the bottom of Granny's apron. Making peach preserves, rolling out biscuit dough, and getting a lick off the spoon were part of life.

My dad always entertained anyone who dropped by, my grandfather grew figs and made fig preserves, and my sisters loved to bake. We now all get together at Thanksgiving for some fellowship and an amazing spread of food. It's my favorite time of year.

Music and food are the lifelines of the South. I started sharing my passion for both when I opened a restaurant in the Lake Oconee area of Georgia, where I could cook and perform in the same spot.

That led me to start taking Cookie, a mobile industrial kitchen inside a tractor-trailer, on the road with the band when we perform. We use it to feed a gourmet meal to up to 150 fans before each show. Whatever city we're in, we get fresh ingredients from local farms and markets. From creamed corn to fresh spinach, we serve the best.

These Eat and Greets mean a lot to me. They give me the chance to break bread and share some Southern hospitality with those who love our music. I get to shake hands, sit down, and visit with fans, and they can see all of us in a real light, as real people. It all started at home, and sharing the love on the road through food brings it full circle.

Zac Brown
Frontman of the two-time
Grammy Award-winning Zac Brown Band

Colder Weather
Words and Music by
Zac Brown, Wyatt Durrette,
Levi Lowery and Coy Bowles
Moderately slow
No Hurry
Words and Music by
Zac Brown, Wyatt Durrette
and James Otto
Highway 20 Ride
Chicken Fried
in Mind
Words and Music by
Zac Brown, Wyatt Durrette
and Nic Cowan
LAND SHARK LAGER PRES
ZAC BROWN BAND
WWW.ZACBROWNBAND.COM
GEXA ENERGY PAVILION
RAIN OR SHINE
SAT NOV 12 2011 7:00 PM
LIVE NATION
Zac Brown Band
ing for some - one like you to save me.
Available at musicnotes.com

from the oven

made-from-scratch casseroles, breads, biscuits, and more

garden green bean casserole (pictured on page 129, top)

Homemade croutons and fresh vegetables liven up this long-lived Southern favorite. Put away the can opener, and bring the homegrown flavor to the table.

2 lb. fresh green beans, trimmed and snapped into 1½-inch pieces
2 cups (½-inch) French bread cubes
2 Tbsp. unsalted butter, melted
4½ Tbsp. unsalted butter, divided
1 (8-oz.) package fresh mushrooms, stemmed and quartered
1 medium onion, thinly sliced
1 garlic clove, minced
1 Tbsp. Worcestershire sauce
3 Tbsp. all-purpose flour
1½ cups milk
1 tsp. salt
½ tsp. freshly ground pepper

1. Preheat oven to 375°. Cook beans in boiling water to cover 10 minutes or until fork-tender; drain. Rinse with cold running water; drain. Transfer to a large bowl.
2. Toss bread with melted butter. Arrange in a jelly-roll pan. Bake at 375° for 20 minutes or until crisp.
3. Melt 1½ Tbsp. butter in a large skillet over medium heat. Add mushrooms, and sauté 4 minutes or until mushrooms have browned and liquid has evaporated. Add onion and garlic, and sauté 3 minutes or until tender. Transfer mixture to bowl with beans. Add Worcestershire sauce to warm skillet, stirring to loosen particles from bottom of skillet. Pour sauce over bean mixture.
4. Melt remaining 3 Tbsp. butter over medium-low heat in skillet. Add flour, and cook, stirring constantly, 2 minutes. Slowly add milk; cook, stirring constantly, 3 minutes or until thickened. Stir in salt and pepper.
5. Pour white sauce over bean mixture. Stir until well blended, and transfer to a lightly greased 11- x 7-inch baking dish. Top with toasted bread cubes. Bake at 375° for 15 minutes or until lightly browned.
Makes: 6 to 8 servings Hands-on Time: 30 min.
Total Time: 1 hr., 15 min.

roasted cauliflower gratin (pictured on page 129, bottom)

Roasting cauliflower turns the common steamed vegetable into something extraordinary. Topping it with a creamy white sauce and shredded cheese makes it irresistible.

4 lb. fresh cauliflower
3 Tbsp. extra virgin olive oil
¾ tsp. salt, divided
¾ tsp. freshly ground pepper, divided
2 Tbsp. unsalted butter
2 Tbsp. all-purpose flour
1¼ cups milk
½ tsp. lemon zest
6 oz. sharp Cheddar cheese, shredded (1½ cups)
Garnish: chopped fresh rosemary

1. Preheat oven to 400°. Cut cauliflower into florets, removing stems. (You should have about 1¾ lb. florets.) Wash and pat very dry. Toss together cauliflower, olive oil, ¼ tsp. salt, and ½ tsp. pepper in a large bowl. Divide mixture between 2 jelly-roll pans. Bake at 400° for 38 to 40 minutes or until lightly browned, stirring once halfway through.
2. Melt butter in a heavy saucepan over low heat; whisk in flour until smooth. Cook 1 minute, whisking constantly. Gradually whisk in milk; cook over medium heat, whisking constantly, until mixture is thickened and bubbly (about 2 minutes). Stir in lemon zest and remaining ½ tsp. salt and ¼ tsp. pepper.
3. Preheat broiler with oven rack 5 inches from heat. Arrange roasted cauliflower in a lightly greased 2-qt. gratin dish or a large, shallow ovenproof skillet. Sprinkle half of cheese over cauliflower. Spoon sauce over cheese. Top with remaining cheese. Broil 4 minutes or until browned and bubbly. Garnish, if desired. Serve immediately.
Makes: 8 servings Hands-on Time: 20 min. Total Time: 1 hr., 5 min.

all things sweet potato casserole

(pictured on page 128, bottom)

When I was growing up, the sweet potato casserole landed on the table right beside less kid-friendly foods like Brussels sprouts and green beans. I always thought someone had forgotten that it wasn't time for dessert. I never spoke up to correct the "mistake." I simply devoured as many helpings as I could fit on my plate.

- 4½ cups mashed baked sweet potatoes (about 4 lb. whole)
- 2 large eggs
- ⅔ cup heavy cream
- ⅓ cup firmly packed light brown sugar
- 1 tsp. salt
- 1 tsp. ground cinnamon
- ¼ tsp. ground nutmeg
- ¾ cup unsalted butter, melted and divided
- 1½ cups crushed gingersnaps (30 cookies)
- 3 cups miniature marshmallows

1. Preheat oven to 350°. Combine potatoes, eggs, next 5 ingredients, and ½ cup melted butter in a large bowl; beat at medium speed with an electric mixer until smooth. Spoon into a lightly greased 13- x 9-inch baking dish.
2. Stir remaining ¼ cup melted butter into crushed gingersnaps. Top potato mixture with marshmallows and the gingersnap mixture in alternating crosswise rows.
3. Bake at 350° for 28 minutes or until marshmallows are lightly browned.
Makes: 12 servings Hands-on Time: 20 min. Total Time: 1 hr., 33 min.

Note: To bake sweet potatoes, place on a baking sheet. Bake at 375° until tender, about 45 minutes for small potatoes, 1 hour for medium potatoes, or 1 hour and 15 minutes to 1 hour and 25 minutes for large potatoes.

signature pieces: trivets
Originally made to elevate cooking pots from the hot coals in the fireplace, early trivets had long handles and legs and were often made from wrought iron. As oven baking replaced fireplace cooking, trivets evolved. They now serve primarily to protect tabletops or tablecloths from the heat of hot dishes.

Trivet materials range from brass to silicone. Shapes and color choices are nearly endless. Some cooks hang trivets on the wall for decoration when not in use. They are especially important during family-style suppers across the South, where casseroles and cast-iron skillets come hot to the table.

down-home squash soufflé

(pictured on page 128, top)

A soufflé in the South is not necessarily a puffed creation involving egg whites. Often, it's simply a casserole. Squash soufflé has been a staple at potlucks and church suppers for generations. To prevent sogginess, I always steam the squash rather than boil it.

2 lb. yellow squash, cut into ½-inch-thick slices
2 Tbsp. unsalted butter
1 medium onion, chopped
½ cup mayonnaise
⅓ cup heavy cream
¼ cup sour cream
¾ tsp. salt
¼ tsp. freshly ground pepper
6 oz. sharp Cheddar cheese, shredded (1½ cups)
35 round, buttery crackers, crushed

1. Arrange squash in a steamer basket over boiling water. Cover and steam 12 to 16 minutes or until fork-tender. Cool 15 minutes.
2. Preheat oven to 350°. Melt butter in a small skillet. Add onion; sauté 5 minutes or until tender. Transfer to a bowl. Stir in mayonnaise, next 4 ingredients, and 1 cup cheese until well blended. Add squash and crushed crackers; stir well. Pour mixture into a lightly greased 8-inch square baking dish, and top with remaining ½ cup cheese.
3. Bake at 350° for 35 minutes or until lightly browned.

Makes: 8 to 10 servings Hands-on Time: 25 min.
Total Time: 1 hr., 30 min.

creamed oysters with spinach

I owe my love of creamy baked oysters to my hometown next-door neighbor. Becky Rawlins made enchanting scalloped oysters and thankfully shared her recipe with Mama. We were lucky enough to enjoy it each Christmas. My version of this rich casserole mirrors Oysters Rockefeller. It's just as fabulous and much easier to eat.

¼ cup unsalted butter, divided
1¼ cups chopped onion
2 (6-oz.) packages fresh baby spinach
2 pt. fresh oysters, very well drained
3 Tbsp. all-purpose flour
1½ cups whipping cream
½ cup freshly grated Parmigiano-Reggiano cheese
¼ tsp. ground red pepper
½ tsp. salt
1⅔ cups soft, fresh breadcrumbs
2 Tbsp. unsalted butter, melted

1. Melt 1 Tbsp. butter in a large skillet over medium heat. Add onion; cook 4 minutes or until tender. Add spinach, and cook, stirring constantly, 2 minutes or until spinach is wilted. Add oysters. Cook, stirring occasionally, 4 minutes or just until edges begin curl.
2. Melt remaining 3 Tbsp. butter in a Dutch oven over medium heat. Add flour. Cook, stirring constantly, 1 minute. Gradually add whipping cream. Cook, stirring frequently, 7 minutes or until thickened. Add cheese and next 2 ingredients, stirring until cheese is melted.
3. Transfer oyster mixture to cheese sauce using a slotted spoon.
4. Preheat broiler with oven rack 6 inches from heat. Arrange ⅔ cup breadcrumbs in a lightly greased 2-qt. baking dish. Add oyster mixture. Top with remaining 1 cup breadcrumbs. Drizzle with 2 Tbsp. melted butter. Broil 4 minutes or until browned.
Makes: 8 to 10 servings Hands-on Time: 35 min. Total Time: 40 min.

puffed chicken pot pie

You can make this classic comfort food in one large baking dish, but putting it in miniature skillets raises it to a level fit for company. Either way, make sure the filling is hot and the pastry is cold when it goes in the oven.

¾	lb. carrots
2	celery ribs
1	yellow onion
2	Tbsp. extra virgin olive oil
1	tsp. freshly ground pepper, divided
¾	tsp. salt, divided
6	Tbsp. unsalted butter
6	Tbsp. all-purpose flour
3	cups chicken broth
4	cups chopped roasted or rotisserie chicken
1½	cups sweet peas (if frozen, thaw)
1	tsp. fresh thyme leaves, chopped, plus sprigs for garnish
1	large egg
½	(17.3-oz.) package frozen puff pastry sheets, thawed but cold

1. Preheat oven to 400°. Cut carrots and celery into ½-inch-thick slices. Cut onion into quarters. Arrange on a jelly-roll pan. Toss with olive oil; sprinkle with ½ tsp. pepper and ¼ tsp. salt. Bake at 400° for 55 minutes or until tender and lightly browned.
2. Melt butter in a large Dutch oven over low heat; whisk in flour until smooth. Cook 1 minute, whisking constantly. Gradually whisk in chicken broth; cook over medium heat, whisking constantly, 5 minutes or until mixture is slightly thickened.
3. Cut roasted onion into bite-size pieces and add to Dutch oven. Stir roasted carrots and celery, chicken, next 2 ingredients, and remaining ½ tsp. pepper and ½ tsp. salt into broth mixture. Cook, stirring often, 10 minutes or until thickened and bubbly. Pour into a lightly greased 13- x 9-inch baking dish.
4. Whisk together egg and 1 Tbsp. water in a small bowl. Roll puff pastry sheet into a 15- x 12-inch rectangle on a lightly floured surface. Arrange pastry over hot filling; trim off excess, tuck edges in, and seal to edge of dish. Brush pastry with egg mixture using a pastry brush. Cut 5 to 6 slits in top of pastry to allow steam to escape.
5. Bake at 400° for 40 minutes or until pastry is golden brown. Garnish, if desired.

Makes: 8 to 10 servings Hands-on Time: 36 min. Total Time: 2 hr.

Note: For appetizer-size pot pies, arrange 12 lightly greased 3½-inch cast-iron skillets on an aluminum foil-lined baking sheet. Spoon a scant ½ cup of hot filling into each skillet. Cut puff pastry into 12 (approximately 4-inch) squares and lay 1 atop each skillet. Brush pastry with egg mixture, and cut slits in tops. Bake at 400° for 20 minutes or until pastry is golden brown.

hoppin' john bake

Hoppin' John is on many a Southern table on New Year's Day, but I think it's too good to just enjoy one day of the year. Bake it with Monterey Jack cheese, and have an extra helping of luck all year-round.

½ (16-oz.) package dried black-eyed peas
4 cups chicken broth, plus additional for rice
1 cup uncooked long-grain rice
3 bacon slices
1 red bell pepper, finely chopped
1 yellow onion, finely chopped
2 garlic cloves, minced
½ tsp. salt
¼ tsp. freshly ground pepper
8 oz. Monterey Jack cheese

1. Rinse and sort peas according to package directions. Cover with water 3 inches above peas; let soak 8 hours. Drain and rinse well.
2. Combine peas and 4 cups broth. Bring to a boil; cover and simmer 1 hour and 30 minutes. Meanwhile, cook rice according to package directions, using chicken broth instead of water.
3. Cook bacon in a skillet over medium heat, turning once, 5 minutes or until crisp. Remove bacon, and drain on paper towels, reserving 2 Tbsp. drippings in skillet. Crumble bacon. Cook bell pepper and next 2 ingredients in hot drippings, stirring often, 10 minutes. Transfer to a large bowl. Stir in salt and pepper.
4. Preheat oven to 350°. Grate cheese on the large holes of a box grater.
5. Remove black-eyed peas from broth using a slotted spoon. (You should have about 3 cups peas.) Discard broth. Add peas to bell pepper mixture. Add rice, crumbled bacon, and 1 cup cheese. Stir gently to combine. Transfer to a lightly greased 11- x 7-inch baking dish or divide among 6 lightly greased (10-oz.) ramekins. Top with remaining cheese.
6. Bake at 350° for 15 minutes or until cheese is melted. Serve immediately.
Makes: 6 servings Hands-on Time: 45 min. Total Time: 9 hr., 50 min.

blue crab casserole (pictured on facing page, top right)

In this rich casserole, crab cooks to bubbly perfection with white wine, sweet onion, and fresh corn. Serve it either as a satisfying main course or a memorable side.

1 (1-inch) slice fresh challah bread or 1 (2-inch) slice French bread
2 Tbsp. unsalted butter
1½ cups diced Vidalia onion
½ cup diced celery
½ cup chopped green onions
¼ cup diced red bell pepper
2 cups fresh corn kernels (4 ears)
½ cup dry white wine
1¼ cups heavy cream
1 lb. fresh lump blue crabmeat, picked and drained
1 Tbsp. chopped fresh parsley
2 Tbsp. fresh lemon juice (about 1 lemon)
½ tsp. salt
½ tsp. hot sauce
¼ tsp. freshly ground pepper
2 Tbsp. unsalted butter, melted

1. Preheat oven to 350°. Process challah in a food processor until finely crumbled. You should have ¾ cup breadcrumbs.
2. Melt 2 Tbsp. butter in a large skillet over medium heat. Add onion and next 3 ingredients. Cook, stirring often, 6 minutes. Add corn, and cook, stirring often, 4 minutes or until lightly browned. Stir in wine; cook 2 minutes or until wine has almost completely evaporated. Add cream; cook 4 minutes or until slightly thickened. Stir in crab and next 5 ingredients. Cook 2 minutes. Pour into a lightly greased 8-inch square baking dish.
3. Toss breadcrumbs with 2 Tbsp. melted butter, and sprinkle over top of crab mixture. Bake at 350° for 20 minutes or until lightly browned and bubbly.
Makes: 6 main-dish or 10 side-dish servings Hands-on Time: 35 min.
Total Time: 55 min.

macaroni with five cheeses

(pictured on page 140, bottom right)

I rarely meet a macaroni and cheese I don't like. For me, it's a dish that makes the world a better place. With five cheeses and toasted croissants on top, comfort food doesn't get more luxurious than this.

1 (16-oz.) package elbow macaroni
2 (2-oz.) croissants, cut into ½-inch cubes
3 oz. sharp Cheddar cheese
3 oz. sharp white Cheddar cheese
2 oz. provolone cheese
1 oz. Asiago cheese
1 oz. Parmigiano-Reggiano cheese
½ cup unsalted butter
½ cup all-purpose flour
4 cups milk
2 tsp. salt
½ tsp. freshly ground pepper

1. Preheat oven to 350°. Prepare macaroni according to package directions.
2. Arrange croissant cubes in a jelly-roll pan. Bake at 350° for 6 minutes or until lightly browned.
3. Grate all cheeses using the large holes of a box grater.
4. Melt butter in a heavy saucepan over low heat; whisk in flour until smooth. Cook 1 minute, whisking constantly. Gradually whisk in milk; cook over medium heat, whisking constantly, 5 minutes or until mixture is thickened and bubbly. Add cheeses, salt, and pepper; stir until cheeses melt. Stir in macaroni.
5. Spoon mixture into a lightly greased 13- x 9-inch baking dish. (Dish will be full.) Sprinkle croissant cubes over macaroni. Bake at 350° for 20 minutes or until macaroni is thoroughly heated and croissant cubes are golden brown.
Makes: 8 to 10 servings **Hands-on Time: 30 min.** **Total Time: 1 hr.**

virginia's winter greens-and-butternut squash gratin (pictured on page 140, left)

The first time I tasted this incredible recipe, it was made with collard greens instead of kale. My dear friend Virginia Willis cooked it for an event we did together, and the audience oohed and aahed over every forkful. This year, it was a hit on my Thanksgiving menu. It's all my favorite cold-weather flavors packed into one beautiful dish.

3 lb. butternut squash
6 cups chopped fresh kale
6 garlic cloves, minced
2 Tbsp. extra virgin olive oil
½ tsp. kosher salt, divided
½ tsp. freshly ground pepper, divided
2 tsp. chopped fresh thyme
½ tsp. freshly grated nutmeg
Pinch of ground allspice
1½ cups heavy cream
3 Tbsp. soft, fresh breadcrumbs
⅔ cup freshly grated Parmigiano-Reggiano cheese
2 tsp. unsalted butter

1. Preheat oven to 400°. Cut squash in half lengthwise; seed, peel, and cut crosswise into ¼-inch slices.
2. Bring a large pot of salted water to a rolling boil. Add kale, and cook 5 minutes or just until tender. Drain well; squeeze out any excess water.
3. Cook garlic and kale in hot oil in a large skillet over medium-high heat 3 minutes or until kale is slightly wilted. Stir in ⅛ tsp. salt and ⅛ tsp. pepper.
4. Place half of squash in a lightly greased 13- x 9-inch baking dish or gratin dish. Season with ⅛ tsp. salt and ⅛ tsp. pepper. Arrange kale mixture over squash. Combine thyme, nutmeg, and allspice in a small bowl. Sprinkle half of thyme mixture over kale. Top with remaining squash; sprinkle with remaining thyme mixture.
5. Heat cream in a heavy nonaluminum saucepan over medium heat, stirring often, 4 to 5 minutes or just until bubbles appear (do not boil); remove from heat. Pour cream over thyme mixture, and cover with aluminum foil.
6. Bake at 400° for 25 minutes; uncover and press mixture down to compress using a spatula. Cover and bake 20 more minutes or until squash is soft when pierced with a knife. Meanwhile, combine breadcrumbs, cheese, and the remaining ¼ tsp. salt and ¼ tsp. pepper in a small bowl.
7. Decrease oven temperature to 375°. Uncover casserole, and sprinkle with breadcrumb mixture. Dot with butter, and bake, uncovered, 10 minutes or until golden brown. Transfer to a wire rack, and let cool 10 minutes before serving.
Makes: 12 servings Hands-on Time: 30 min. Total Time: 1 hr., 45 min.

chicken and dressing

For me, the highlight of Thanksgiving is sitting down to a perfectly roasted turkey and my grandmother Tom's dressing. At other times of year, I like to make an all-in-one chicken version for a comforting supper. The cornbread recipe makes a little more than you'll need for the dressing. For a cook's snack, slather the extra with butter, and eat it warm right out of the skillet.

2 Tbsp. unsalted butter
½ cup diced white onion
½ cup diced celery
2 garlic cloves, minced
4 cups crumbled Family Cornbread
3 cups chicken broth
6 white bread slices, torn into 1-inch pieces
4 Tbsp. unsalted butter, melted
2 large eggs
1 Tbsp. dried sage
1 tsp. salt
½ tsp. freshly ground pepper
4 cups shredded roasted or rotisserie chicken

1. Preheat oven to 375°. Melt 2 Tbsp. butter in a large skillet over medium heat. Add onion and next 2 ingredients. Cook, stirring frequently, 10 minutes or until softened and beginning to brown. Transfer to a large bowl. Add crumbled cornbread and next 7 ingredients. Let stand 15 minutes.
2. Spoon about one-third cornbread mixture into a lightly greased 13- x 9-inch baking dish. Arrange chicken over cornbread mixture. Top with remaining cornbread mixture. Bake at 375° for 45 minutes or until golden brown and set.
Makes: 8 to 10 servings Hands-on Time: 30 min.
Total Time: 2 hr., 25 min., including cornbread

family cornbread

3 Tbsp. bacon drippings
1 large egg
1 cup milk
1 cup self-rising white cornmeal mix
½ cup self-rising soft-wheat flour (such as White Lily)

1. Preheat oven to 500°. Place bacon drippings in a 10-inch cast-iron skillet; heat in oven 4 minutes. Meanwhile, whisk together egg and milk in a small bowl. Whisk together cornmeal mix and flour in a medium bowl; gently whisk in egg mixture.
2. Remove skillet from oven; carefully pour half of hot drippings into batter. (Drippings will sizzle.) Whisk to combine. Pour batter into skillet.
3. Bake at 500° for 13 minutes or until golden brown and cornbread pulls away from sides of skillet. Let cool 30 minutes.
Makes: 8 to 10 servings Hands-on Time: 10 min. Total Time: 55 min.

chicken and wild rice with pecans

Everyone seems to have a version of chicken-and-rice casserole. It's a universal comfort food, no matter where you grew up. I like the texture of the pecans on top of this casserole and the sophistication of leeks and white Cheddar.

1 cup uncooked long-grain and wild rice mix (such as RiceSelect Royal Blend Texmati white, brown, red, and wild rice blend)
1 leek
2 Tbsp. unsalted butter
1 (16-oz.) package fresh mushrooms, stemmed and quartered
½ cup dry white wine
4 cups shredded roasted or rotisserie chicken
1 cup sour cream
1 tsp. salt
½ tsp. freshly ground pepper
2 oz. white Cheddar cheese, shredded (½ cup)
½ cup coarsely chopped pecans
Garnish: chopped chives

1. Cook wild rice blend according to package directions.
2. Meanwhile, remove and discard root, tough outer layers, and top from leek, leaving white portion and 3 inches of dark green portion. Cut into quarters lengthwise. Thinly slice leek; rinse well, and drain.
3. Preheat oven to 350°. Melt butter in a large skillet over medium-low heat. Add leek, and cook 6 to 7 minutes or until lightly browned. Add mushrooms, and cook, stirring often, 15 minutes. Add wine, and bring to a simmer; cook 3 minutes.
4. Transfer rice to a large bowl. Add leek mixture to rice; stir until blended. Add chicken and next 3 ingredients; stir until blended. Transfer to a lightly greased 11- x 7-inch baking dish. Top with cheese.
5. Bake at 350° for 10 minutes. Top with pecans; bake 10 more minutes or until pecans are toasted and mixture is bubbly. Garnish, if desired.
Makes: 6 servings   Hands-on Time: 45 min.   Total Time: 1 hr., 5 min.

bacon-and-swiss bread pudding

(pictured on facing page, right)

Bread puddings are often thought of as dessert, but this savory version is right at home beside big steaks or roast chicken. I can't think of a better way to transform stale bread into something magnificent.

1 lb. thick-cut bacon slices, chopped
2 cups half-and-half
4 large eggs
8 cups (2-day-old) sourdough bread cubes (1-inch cubes)
2 cups quartered and thinly sliced white onion
2 garlic cloves, minced
⅓ cup dry white wine
1½ tsp. chopped fresh thyme
½ tsp. freshly ground pepper
8 oz. Swiss cheese, shredded (2 cups)

1. Preheat oven to 350°. Cook bacon in a large skillet over medium heat 16 minutes or until crisp. Remove bacon with a slotted spoon, reserving 3 Tbsp. drippings in skillet. Reserve remaining drippings for another use.
2. Whisk together half-and-half and eggs in a large bowl. Add bread cubes; let stand 10 minutes.
3. Meanwhile, add onion and garlic to hot drippings in skillet. Cook over medium heat, stirring frequently, 6 minutes or until tender. Add wine, and cook 2 minutes, stirring to loosen particles from bottom of skillet. Add onion mixture to bread mixture, and stir until blended. Add bacon, thyme, pepper, and 1¼ cups cheese. Stir until blended. Transfer to a lightly greased 11- x 7-inch baking dish. Top with remaining cheese.
4. Bake at 350° for 45 minutes or until puffed and golden.

Makes: 8 to 10 servings   Hands-on Time: 40 min.
Total Time: 1 hr., 35 min.

cornbread sticks (pictured on page 148, bottom left)

Perfect for chili and soups, these crisp-tender buttermilk cornbread sticks are a favorite of many Southern childhoods. With only a few minutes needed to bake a batch, there's no excuse to go without fresh cornbread. Try them with butter and honey for a sweet-savory snack.

1 cup stone-ground white cornmeal (such as McEwen & Sons)
½ cup all-purpose soft-wheat flour (such as White Lily)
½ tsp. salt
½ tsp. baking powder
¼ tsp. ground red pepper (optional)
1 cup buttermilk
2 large eggs
¼ cup unsalted butter, melted
Vegetable oil

1. Preheat oven to 450°. Heat 2 (7-well) cast-iron corn stick pans in oven 5 minutes.
2. Meanwhile, whisk together cornmeal, next 3 ingredients, and, if desired, red pepper in a large bowl. Whisk together buttermilk and eggs in a small bowl, and add to cornmeal mixture, whisking until blended. Stir in melted butter.
3. Lightly brush corn stick pans with vegetable oil. Pour batter into hot pans. Bake at 450° for 15 minutes or until golden brown. Serve warm.

Makes: 14 sticks Hands-on Time: 10 min. Total Time: 25 min.

Note: I use Lodge cast-iron pans with 7 wells that are shaped like ears of corn. You can find them at retail stores or online at lodgemfg.com. Pans are available in 5-, 7-, and 9-well versions, as well as miniature. If you have only one pan, bake the batter in batches, brushing the pan with oil between each batch.

buttermilk hush puppies stuffed with pimiento cheese

(pictured on page 148, top left)

No fish fry is complete without piping-hot hush puppies. Finding melted pimiento cheese in the middle of them is like finding stray money in the bottom of your purse. You don't expect it but are oh-so-happy it's there.

4 oz. sharp Cheddar cheese
1 Tbsp. mayonnaise
1 (2-oz.) jar diced pimiento, drained
Vegetable oil
2½ cups self-rising buttermilk cornmeal mix
1 cup finely chopped onion
1 tsp. sugar
1¼ cups buttermilk
1 large egg

1. Grate cheese on the large holes of a box grater. Combine cheese, mayonnaise, and pimiento in a bowl.
2. Pour oil to depth of 2 inches into a Dutch oven; heat to 375°.
3. Combine cornmeal mix and next 2 ingredients in a large bowl. Whisk together buttermilk and egg in a small bowl. Add buttermilk mixture to cornmeal mixture, stirring just until dry ingredients are moistened.
4. Spoon out a scant tablespoonful of dough using a measuring spoon. Top with 1 tsp. pimiento cheese. Cover with another scant tablespoonful of dough, and use your fingers to mold it around cheese on all sides. Repeat procedure with remaining dough and pimiento cheese.
5. Carefully drop stuffed hush puppies into hot oil, and fry about 1½ minutes on each side or until lightly browned. Serve immediately.

Makes: 22 servings **Hands-on Time:** 40 min. **Total Time:** 40 min.

country ham-and-cheese biscuit bread

Imagine a biscuit already loaded with gooey cheese and salty country ham, and you get this all-in-one bread. Layering the dough in a loaf pan lets you get all that Southern goodness in every bite.

6 oz. country ham
1 Tbsp. unsalted butter
4 oz. Cheddar cheese
3½ cups self-rising soft-wheat flour (such as White Lily), divided
½ cup unsalted butter, cut into ½-inch cubes
1 cup buttermilk
1 Tbsp. unsalted butter, melted

1. Preheat oven to 400°. Cut ham into ½-inch pieces. Melt 1 Tbsp. butter in a large skillet over medium heat. Add ham; sauté 4 minutes or until lightly browned. Transfer ham to a small bowl; chill.
2. Grate cheese on the large holes of a box grater, and chill.
3. Pulse 3 cups flour and ½ cup cubed butter in a food processor 8 times, using the metal blade. Add buttermilk; process until a dough forms.
4. Transfer dough to a well-floured surface. Use floured hands to knead in remaining ½ cup flour; knead until dough is smooth and elastic (about 2 minutes). Divide dough in half. Roll each half into a (16- x 4-inch) rectangle. Cut each rectangle in half crosswise. (You should have 4 rectangles about the size of your loaf pan.)
5. Place 1 dough rectangle in an ungreased 8½- x 4½-inch loaf pan, patting dough to edges of pan. Top with one-third of ham, pressing very lightly to adhere. Sprinkle with one-third of cheese. Repeat layers two more times, patting each dough layer to edges of pan. Top with remaining portion of dough. Brush with 1 Tbsp. melted butter.
6. Bake at 400° for 35 to 40 minutes or until golden brown. Cool in pan on a wire rack 25 minutes. Serve warm or at room temperature.
Makes: 1 loaf Hands-on Time: 30 min. Total Time: 1 hr., 30 min.

cloverleaf yeast rolls (pictured on facing page, center)

It's hard not to fall in love with the warm, buttery comfort of a homemade yeast roll. With two small children running in and out of the kitchen, I'm always looking for inventive places to stash the dough so that it's warm and undisturbed as it rises. Rise times will vary, depending on the heat and stillness of the spot you choose.

1 (¼-oz.) envelope active dry yeast
¼ cup warm water (105° to 115°)
½ cup milk
3 Tbsp. unsalted butter
½ cup buttermilk, at room temperature
2 Tbsp. sugar
1 Tbsp. honey
1 tsp. salt
1 large egg, lightly beaten
4 cups sifted all-purpose flour
2 Tbsp. unsalted butter, melted and divided
Additional butter, softened

1. Combine yeast and warm water in a small bowl. Let stand 5 minutes.
2. Heat milk and 3 Tbsp. butter in a small saucepan over medium heat until butter is melted and mixture begins to steam. Pour into bowl of a heavy-duty electric stand mixer. Stir in buttermilk, sugar, honey, and salt. Cool to between 105° and 115° (about 5 minutes). Add yeast mixture and egg, and beat at low speed, using dough hook attachment, just until blended. Add flour, and beat at medium speed 3 minutes or until a smooth dough forms.
3. Turn dough out onto a well-floured surface, and knead 30 seconds using floured hands. (Dough will be very soft.) Coat a large bowl with 1 Tbsp. melted butter. Place dough in bowl, turning to grease top. Cover dough with plastic wrap, and let rise in a warm place (85°), free from drafts, 1 hour or until doubled in bulk.
4. Punch dough down. Turn out onto a lightly floured surface, and shape into 72 (1-inch) balls. Place 3 balls in each cup of 2 lightly greased (12-cup) muffin pans. Cover and let rise in a warm place (85°), free from drafts, 1 hour or until doubled in bulk.
5. Preheat oven to 375°. Brush tops of rolls with remaining 1 Tbsp. melted butter. Bake at 375° for 18 minutes or until lightly browned. Serve immediately with softened butter.
Makes: 24 servings Hands-on Time: 35 min. Total Time: 3 hr.

itsy-bitsy cream cheese biscuits (pictured on page 154, left)

These one-bite biscuits are so buttery and creamy they don't need any butter. Serve them hot out of the oven as a before-dinner snack or as an addition to an appetizer buffet.

1 cup self-rising soft-wheat flour (such as White Lily)
⅓ cup unsalted butter, softened
6 oz. cream cheese, softened
2 Tbsp. milk

1. Pulse flour, butter, and cream cheese in a food processor until dough begins to come together, using the metal blade. Add milk. Pulse 4 times or until milk is absorbed. Remove dough from bowl, wrap in plastic wrap, and chill 45 minutes.
2. Preheat oven to 425°. Unwrap dough, and place on a well-floured surface. Knead 4 to 5 times or until dough is smooth and does not have any lumps. Pat to ⅓-inch thickness. Cut with a well-floured 1½-inch round cutter. (Be very careful not to twist the cutter.) Combine any dough scraps, pat to ⅓-inch thickness, and cut into rounds. Place rounds on an ungreased, light-colored baking sheet.
3. Bake at 425° for 12 minutes or until tops are slightly golden. Serve warm or at room temperature.
Makes: 22 biscuits **Hands-on Time:** 20 min. **Total Time:** 1 hr., 20 min.

angel biscuits (pictured on page 154, right)

Angel biscuits are sometimes called "bride's biscuits" because they are virtually foolproof, even for novice cooks. With the leavening plus the yeast, these biscuits are bound to be fluffy. The dough can be stored in the fridge for several days, so the biscuits can be baked when needed and enjoyed in small quantities.

1 (¼-oz.) envelope active dry yeast
3 Tbsp. warm water (105° to 115°)
⅓ cup sugar, divided
5 cups self-rising soft-wheat flour (such as White Lily)
½ cup shortening
½ cup cold unsalted butter, cut into ½-inch cubes
1¾ cups buttermilk
Additional butter, softened (optional)

1. Combine yeast, warm water, and 1 tsp. sugar in a small bowl; let stand 5 minutes or until foamy.
2. Whisk together flour and remaining 5 Tbsp. sugar in a large bowl; cut in shortening and cubed butter with a pastry blender or fork until crumbly. Stir in yeast mixture and buttermilk, stirring just until dry ingredients are moistened. Turn dough out onto a lightly floured surface, and knead 5 times. Place dough in a large bowl, cover with plastic wrap, and chill 8 hours or up to 5 days.
3. Turn dough out onto a lightly floured surface. Knead dough 8 times. Roll to ½-inch thickness. Cut with a 2¼-inch round cutter. Reroll and cut dough scraps once (discard any remaining scraps). Arrange biscuits, with sides touching, on an ungreased baking sheet.
4. Cover baking sheet loosely with plastic wrap. Let rise in a warm place (85°), free from drafts, until doubled in bulk, about 1½ hours.
5. Preheat oven to 400°. Bake 16 to 18 minutes or until golden. Serve warm with softened butter, if desired.
Makes: 32 biscuits Hands-on Time: 20 min. Total Time: 10 hr.

cat-head biscuits with tomato gravy

Cat-head biscuits are delightfully huge, crispy-on-the-outside, fluffy-on-the-inside homemade biscuits. Their size and crunch make them ideal to serve with a thick, hearty gravy. The name comes from their colossal size, about that of a cat's head. They bake longer and at a lower temperature than their smaller cousins. If you don't have bacon drippings on hand, cook a pound of bacon before you start this recipe, reserve the drippings, and serve the bacon with the biscuits and gravy.

5 Tbsp. warm bacon drippings
5 Tbsp. unsalted butter, melted
3½ cups self-rising soft-wheat flour (such as White Lily)
1⅓ cups buttermilk, at room temperature
Parchment paper
Tomato Gravy

1. Preheat oven to 375°. Stir together bacon drippings and butter.
2. Place flour in a large bowl. Stir in drippings mixture and buttermilk, stirring just until a dough forms.
3. Turn dough out onto a well-floured surface. Knead twice. Divide dough into 8 equal portions. Pat each portion into a 3½-inch round biscuit (about ¾ inch thick). Arrange 2 inches apart on a parchment paper-lined baking sheet.
4. Bake at 375° for 30 minutes or until tops are very lightly browned. Meanwhile, prepare Tomato Gravy. Serve biscuits immediately with Tomato Gravy.
Makes: 8 servings Hands-on Time: 15 min.
Total Time: 1 hr., 10 min., including gravy

tomato gravy

2 Tbsp. bacon drippings
1 cup finely chopped Vidalia onion
2 Tbsp. all-purpose soft-wheat flour (such as White Lily)
2 cups peeled, seeded, and finely chopped tomato
½ tsp. salt
¼ tsp. dried thyme
¼ tsp. freshly ground pepper
½ cup milk

1. Heat bacon drippings in a large skillet over medium heat. Add onion, and cook, stirring often, 5 minutes. Sprinkle onion with flour, and cook, stirring constantly, 3 minutes. Add tomato and next 3 ingredients. Cook, stirring often, 6 minutes.
2. Add milk, and bring to a light boil; reduce heat to a simmer, and cook, stirring often, 2 minutes. (If gravy becomes too thick, add more milk for desired consistency.)
Makes: 1½ cups Hands-on Time: 25 min. Total Time: 25 min.

nathalie's yogurt-and-cream biscuits

(pictured on facing page, right)

The one woman who has made the biggest difference in my career is Nathalie Dupree. She took me under her wing and opened the door to a world of food I never imagined existed. She taught me countless lessons, including the real art of making biscuits. Her yogurt-and-cream biscuits are light but tangy, a heavenly combination.

2 cups self-rising soft-wheat flour (such as White Lily)
½ cup plain yogurt
¾ cup heavy cream, divided
Parchment paper
3 Tbsp. unsalted butter, melted

1. Preheat oven to 400°. Whisk flour in a large bowl. Make a well in center of flour. Add yogurt and ½ cup cream. Stir until dough comes together. (Dough will be sticky.) If mixture is dry and flour is not fully incorporated, add remaining ¼ cup cream, 1 Tbsp. at a time, until all the flour is moistened.
2. Turn dough out onto a lightly floured surface. Fold dough in half, and pat into a ½-inch-thick circle using floured hands. Repeat procedure once. Cut dough with a 2-inch round cutter, rerolling dough scraps once. (Be very careful not to twist the cutter. Do not reuse the dough scraps more than once.) Arrange biscuits 2 inches apart on a parchment paper-lined baking sheet.
3. Bake at 400° on top oven rack 10 to 13 minutes or until golden brown. Brush tops with melted butter. Serve immediately.
Makes: 15 biscuits Hands-on Time: 15 min. Total Time: 25 min.

drop-and-cut biscuits (pictured on page 161, bottom left)

These are very casual biscuits that I like more for breakfast than later in the day. They are dropped and cooked shoulder to shoulder in a round cake pan, then cut apart with a spatula. With crisp browned outsides and tender insides, they practically demand to be stuffed with bacon or slathered with jelly.

1¾ cups self-rising soft-wheat flour (such as White Lily)
1 Tbsp. sugar
¼ tsp. salt
⅓ cup shortening
⅓ cup milk
½ cup heavy cream

1. Preheat oven to 450°. Combine flour and next 2 ingredients in a large bowl. Add shortening. Rub shortening into dry ingredients, using your fingers. (Once worked in, you should not see any lumps of shortening in the flour.) Stir in milk and cream.
2. Generously flour your hands. Using 4 fingers like a spoon, scoop out enough dough to cover up to the middle knuckles. Toss the dough back and forth in your hands about 4 times (like the game Hot Potato). Repeat this procedure to make 7 to 10 biscuits, flouring your hands each time and dropping the dough into an ungreased, light-colored 8-inch round cake pan. Arrange the dough like a daisy, with dough balls around the outside edge like petals and 1 or 2 in the center.
3. Bake at 450° for 18 to 20 minutes or until lightly browned. Use a small spatula to cut biscuits and remove from pan. Serve warm.
Makes: 7 to 10 biscuits Hands-on Time: 15 min. Total Time: 35 min.

sweet potato biscuits (pictured on page 161, top left)

Anytime I have leftover baked sweet potatoes, I make a batch of these biscuits. Super-moist and loaded with sweet potato flavor, they're wonderful with ham, blueberry preserves, or butter. A little extra baking powder helps them rise.

1¼ cups buttermilk
1 cup mashed baked sweet potato, at room temperature
4 cups self-rising soft-wheat flour (such as White Lily)
1 Tbsp. baking powder
⅛ tsp. salt
1 cup unsalted butter, cut into ½-inch cubes and chilled
Parchment paper

1. Preheat oven to 425°. Stir together buttermilk and sweet potato in a medium bowl.
2. Combine flour, baking powder, and salt in a large bowl. Cut butter into flour mixture with a pastry blender until it is crumbly and resembles small peas. Add buttermilk mixture, and stir just until dry ingredients are moistened.
3. Turn dough onto a well-floured surface, and knead 4 times with lightly floured hands. Pat dough to ¾-inch thickness. Cut with a 2¾-inch round cutter. (Be very careful not to twist the cutter.) Place biscuits, with sides touching, on a parchment paper-lined baking sheet.
4. Bake at 425° for 20 minutes or until lightly browned.
Makes: 15 biscuits   Hands-on Time: 20 min.   Total Time: 40 min.

table talk:
beaten biscuit brake

Like their namesake tables, beaten biscuits have nearly disappeared from Southern kitchens. The small, unleavened biscuits are pale and nearly flat, more like crackers than traditional biscuits. Old recipes call for the dough to be kneaded for hours or to be vigorously beaten hundreds of times with a rolling pin or a skillet.

The beaten biscuit brake, developed in the late 1800s, provided relief for those who tired of beating their biscuits by hand. This unique contraption involves a crank and two rollers mounted above a heavy slab of marble atop cast-iron legs. The cook threads the dough between the rollers and then cranks until it is smooth. Perhaps owing to the demise of the beaten biscuit itself, these tables are very rare.

herbed buttermilk biscuits

I grew up eating biscuits several times a week. My grandmothers, Tom and Sa, made very different biscuits, each sort divine in its own right. Thanks to Tom, I learned to appreciate the taste of raw biscuit dough as a child, and I still snack on the last little bit of dough scraps. I think both women would be proud of this herbed version—even before it's baked.

- 1½ to 2½ cups self-rising soft-wheat flour (such as White Lily)
- ¼ cup shortening
- ⅔ cup buttermilk
- ¼ cup heavy cream
- 1 Tbsp. assorted chopped fresh herbs (such as thyme, basil, sage, and rosemary)

1. Preheat oven to 450°. Place 1½ cups flour in a large bowl. Add shortening, and use a pinching motion with your fingers to break it up and work it into the flour. (Mixture will be crumbly and resemble small peas.) Add buttermilk and next 2 ingredients, stirring just until flour is moistened.
2. Turn dough out onto a well-floured surface. Using floured hands, knead dough 4 to 5 times by folding dough over and pressing down with the heels of your hands; gradually add as much of remaining flour as needed to make a smooth dough. (The dough should not be sticky.)
3. Pat dough to ¾-inch thickness. Cut with a 2-inch round cutter. (Be very careful not to twist the cutter.) Combine any dough scraps, pat to ¾-inch thickness, and cut into rounds (discard any remaining scraps). Place biscuits, with sides touching, in an ungreased, light-colored jelly-roll pan.
4. Bake at 450° for 16 to 18 minutes or until lightly browned.
Makes: 16 biscuits Hands-on Time: 13 min. Total Time: 30 min.

lace cornbread

This old Southern take on cornbread is a crisp, lacy brown wafer best enjoyed a few seconds after it leaves the skillet. The thin batter spatters and sputters the second it hits the hot pan—that's how the lace is formed. This pretty cornbread was popular in the early twentieth century. Southern kitchens had all the ingredients on hand, and the wafers were inexpensive to make. It's worth the patience to cook them one at a time. Serve them with soup for lunch, with greens at supper, or with preserves as a sweet snack.

½ cup stone-ground white cornmeal
¼ tsp. salt
¼ cup bacon drippings

1. Combine cornmeal, salt, and ¾ cup plus 2 Tbsp. water in a small bowl.
2. Heat 1 heaping Tbsp. bacon drippings in a cast-iron skillet over medium-low heat. When drippings are shimmering (the sign that they're hot), very carefully add 2 Tbsp. batter to hot pan. Gently spread batter from center outward. (The batter will immediately look lacy and bubbly.) Cook 3 minutes or until edges are brown. Turn and cook 3 minutes. Transfer to a wire rack. Repeat procedure with remaining batter, adding more drippings to pan as needed.
Makes: 10 pieces   Hands-on Time: 1 hr., 5 min.
Total Time: 1 hr., 5 min.

my southern table

Our home is a bustling place filled with laughter, love, and lots of spices. With our three young children and Will's little brother growing up fast, the kitchen is often the room where we all come together. The table tends to be covered in homework and school projects right up until dinnertime.

Will was blessed with a grandmother who taught him to cook. Thanks to her lessons and love, he really is a good cook. Like a lot of moms, I started cooking more often after our children were born. My mother and father are both talented in the kitchen. Thanks to growing up in Lafayette, La., I cook with lots of seasonings and spices. I'm a country girl who loves her food hot.

My favorite time to cook is on a night Will calls his "cheat night." Once a week, he takes a break from his nutrition-focused diet, and we cook a big, fun family meal. It's usually on a Wednesday or Thursday, and we splurge and cook whatever we want. My favorite specialties are from my childhood: gumbo, étouffée, crawfish fettuccine, and beef stew. Will sometimes cooks his fried chicken wings or pork chops with gravy. We like it spicy and keep the hot sauce close at hand.

The children love my beef stew and get excited when it's bubbling away on the stove. I have a secret ingredient I use in my stew (and on almost anything else I cook): Italian dressing. I use about 10 bottles a month. If I'm in the kitchen, you can bet Italian dressing is going in a recipe.

No matter the day of the week or who the team is playing next, our family lives life to the fullest and has fun in the kitchen. It's where we eat, study, play, and relax. Our cooking brings us to the table and connects us again and again.

Racquel Smith
Wife of New Orleans Saints defensive end Will Smith
Co-founder of the Where There's a Will, There's a Way foundation

Cajun
Seasoning
TASTES GREAT ON EVERYTHING!
SUPER BOWL XLIV
Champions
Crayon Puzzles
s Missi
f cards should
number.
5
5
4.
0
10
6.
7
3
ost cubes?
D
st cubes?
A
B
C
D

soup spoons & sliced bread

soups, stews, and sandwiches with southern flavor

simple southern oyster stew (pictured on page 171, top)

Oyster stew is one of my dad's favorite meals. Mama makes it often for him, just like my grandmother did for all of us when I was a child. Though it's called stew in the South, it's really a simple, milky oyster soup—the kind you make quickly and cozy up to, with plenty of oyster crackers, on a cold night.

1 pt. fresh standard oysters
4 cups milk
2 cups whipping cream
4 Tbsp. unsalted butter, divided
1 tsp. salt
¾ tsp. hot sauce
½ tsp. freshly ground pepper
1 Tbsp. chopped fresh chives
Oyster crackers

1. Drain oysters, reserving oyster liquor (liquid in oyster container). Pick out and discard bits of shell.
2. Place oyster liquor, milk, whipping cream, and 1 Tbsp. butter in a large, heavy Dutch oven. Cook over medium heat, stirring often, 7 minutes or until butter melts. Scrape bottom and sides of pan to prevent milk from sticking.
3. Meanwhile, melt remaining 3 Tbsp. butter in a medium skillet over medium heat. Add oysters, and cook 2 minutes or until oysters plump up and edges begin to curl. Remove from heat.
4. Add oysters and any liquid in skillet to milk mixture. Stir in salt and next 2 ingredients. Bring to a simmer (do not boil) over medium heat. Remove from heat; let stand, covered, 10 minutes. Season with more salt, pepper, and hot sauce to taste.
5. Ladle hot stew into soup bowls. Sprinkle with chives, and serve with oyster crackers.

Makes: 8 cups Hands-on Time: 25 min. Total Time: 40 min.

tomato-and-roasted red pepper soup with cheddar croutons (pictured on page 171, bottom)

There's no other soup I'd rather dip my spoon into than a bowl of homemade tomato soup. Adding a roasted red bell pepper deepens the color and brings a new dimension to the taste. Once you've had the cheesy croutons on top, you may never serve naked soup again.

1 red bell pepper
2½ lb. tomatoes, cut into 2-inch pieces
¾ lb. Vidalia onions, cut into 2-inch pieces
2 garlic cloves
2 Tbsp. extra virgin olive oil
¾ tsp. salt, divided
¾ tsp. freshly ground black pepper, divided
4 cups chicken broth
4 oz. French bread, cut into ¾-inch cubes
2 Tbsp. unsalted butter, melted
1 oz. sharp Cheddar cheese, shredded (¼ cup)
Garnish: fresh basil leaves

1. Preheat oven to 500°. Place bell pepper on an aluminum foil-lined baking sheet, and bake, turning 4 times, for 45 minutes or until bell pepper looks blistered. Place bell pepper in a zip-top plastic freezer bag; seal and let stand 10 minutes. Peel, remove and discard seeds, and coarsely chop.
2. Reduce oven temperature to 450°. Arrange tomato and onion in a jelly-roll pan. Add garlic and olive oil, and toss to coat. Sprinkle with ½ tsp. each salt and black pepper. Bake at 450° for 45 minutes. Cool 15 minutes.
3. Transfer roasted bell pepper and tomato and onion mixture to a food processor bowl. Process 2 minutes or until smooth. Transfer to a Dutch oven, and add chicken broth. Bring to a boil over medium heat; reduce heat, and simmer 30 minutes or until thickened.
4. Toss bread pieces in melted butter. Sprinkle with cheese and remaining ¼ tsp. each salt and black pepper. Arrange in a jelly-roll pan. Bake at 450° for 5 minutes or until crisp.
5. Serve soup with croutons. Garnish, if desired.

Makes: 6 cups Hands-on Time: 20 min. Total Time: 2 hr., 15 min.

rich corn chowder (pictured on page 170, bottom)

You don't have to drive far in any direction in South Georgia to be surrounded by cornfields. Summertime means corn is coming. When it arrives, we eat it nearly every day. I think ahead to winter and freeze as much as room allows. I'm always warmed by summer corn in a bowl on a cold January night.

- 5 thick-cut bacon slices, chopped
- 2 cups chopped onion
- 1 cup chopped celery
- 3 garlic cloves, minced
- 1 jalapeño pepper, diced
- 4 cups frozen whole kernel corn, thawed
- 3 cups chicken broth
- 1 tsp. salt
- ¼ tsp. freshly ground black pepper
- 1 cup half-and-half
- 1 avocado, peeled and chopped
- 1 cup grape tomatoes, quartered
- ¼ cup chopped fresh flat-leaf parsley

1. Cook bacon in a large skillet over medium heat, stirring often, 12 minutes or until crisp. Remove with a slotted spoon, and drain on paper towels.
2. Carefully pour hot drippings through a fine wire-mesh strainer into a large Dutch oven; heat drippings over medium heat. Cook onion and next 3 ingredients in hot drippings, stirring occasionally, 7 minutes or until tender. (Do not brown onion.) Add corn; cook, stirring occasionally, 5 minutes. Add chicken broth, salt, and black pepper. Bring to a boil; reduce heat to low, and simmer 30 minutes. Remove from heat.
3. Process mixture with a handheld blender until almost all of mixture is mostly pureed. (Leave a few kernels whole.) Stir in half-and-half. Cook over low heat 3 minutes or until thoroughly heated. Serve with bacon, avocado, tomato, and parsley.

Makes: 7 cups Hands-on Time: 40 min. Total Time: 1 hr., 15 min.

signature pieces: soup tureens
Tureens can range from elaborately adorned to simply elegant. On tables around the world for more than 300 years, tureens are a functional blending of art and practicality.

Most soup tureens are large covered bowls with matching platters and ladles. The covers are conveniently notched so that the ladle can remain in the bowl at all times. Tureens can be used to hold bisques, broths, soups, and stews. They also make excellent stand-ins for proper punch bowls.

caramelized vidalia soup with crispy sage

(pictured on page 170, top)

In this soup, a mound of sweet onions takes its sweet time cooking down to caramelized goodness. Be patient, and don't add the wine until the onions are richly colored. I like to use my biggest Le Creuset pot. If you don't have a large enameled cast-iron Dutch oven, divide the butter and onions between your two largest, widest, heavy-bottomed skillets to help the onions caramelize rather than steam.

½ cup unsalted butter
6 lb. Vidalia onions, cut into ¼-inch-thick rings (14 cups rings)
½ cup dry red wine (such as Pinot Noir)
½ tsp. salt
½ tsp. freshly ground pepper
4 cups chicken broth
¼ cup heavy cream
1 Tbsp. extra virgin olive oil
15 fresh sage leaves

1. Melt butter in a 12- to 15-inch-wide enameled cast-iron Dutch oven over medium-low heat. Add onions. Cook, stirring occasionally, 1 hour and 45 minutes or until onions are caramel colored.
2. Add wine and next 2 ingredients, stirring to loosen particles from bottom of Dutch oven. Cook 5 minutes. Add chicken broth; cook 10 minutes. Stir in cream.
3. Heat olive oil in a small skillet over medium heat. Add sage, and fry 10 to 30 seconds or until crispy. Remove with a slotted spoon, and drain on paper towels. Top each serving of soup with sage.
Makes: 10 cups   Hands-on Time: 35 min.   Total Time: 2 hr., 20 min.

creamy butternut squash soup

A comforting bowl of butternut squash soup is required eating on chilly days. With just enough red pepper to appreciate and a touch of curry to tease, here's a soup fit for company.

2 large butternut squash (about 2¼ lb. each)
¼ cup extra virgin olive oil, divided
½ tsp. salt
¼ tsp. freshly ground black pepper
1 large sweet onion, chopped
2 garlic cloves, minced
½ tsp. curry powder
⅛ tsp. ground red pepper
3½ cups chicken broth
⅓ cup heavy cream
1 Tbsp. honey
½ tsp. salt
Garnishes: crème fraîche, fresh pomegranate seeds, freshly ground black pepper

1. Preheat oven to 400°. Cut squash in half lengthwise; remove and discard seeds. Arrange, cut sides up, in a jelly-roll pan. Rub cut sides with 2 Tbsp. olive oil. Sprinkle with salt and black pepper.
2. Bake at 400° for 1 hour and 30 minutes or until very tender when pierced with a fork. Cool slightly, and scoop out pulp. Discard peels.
3. Heat remaining 2 Tbsp. olive oil in a Dutch oven over medium heat. Add onion; sauté 7 to 8 minutes or until translucent. Add garlic; sauté 2 minutes. Add squash, curry, and red pepper. Cook, stirring constantly, 2 minutes. Stir in chicken broth.
4. Process mixture with a handheld blender until smooth. Stir in cream and next 2 ingredients. Simmer 5 minutes. Divide among bowls or cups. Garnish, if desired.
Makes: 8 cups Hands-on Time: 40 min. Total Time: 2 hr., 30 min.

georgia shrimp bisque

When I'm near the Georgia coast, I always load up on sweet, local shrimp. This lovely pureed soup weds the best our waters have to offer with rich cream and sherry and creates something voluptuous and extraordinary. Serve it with crusty bread and dry white wine for a filling winter lunch or an elegant first course. You can make the shrimp stock a day ahead.

shrimp stock

- 1½ lb. unpeeled, medium-size raw shrimp
- 2 cups chicken broth
- 1 carrot, quartered
- 1 celery rib, quartered
- 1 small onion, quartered (skin on)
- 4 to 6 fresh flat-leaf parsley sprigs
- ¼ tsp. black peppercorns
- 2 bay leaves

bisque

- 3 Tbsp. unsalted butter
- 1 cup chopped onion
- 2 celery ribs, thinly sliced
- 2 Tbsp. chopped fresh tarragon
- ½ cup dry white wine
- 5 Tbsp. uncooked long-grain rice
- 2 Tbsp. tomato paste
- 2 cups heavy cream
- 1 cup milk
- ½ tsp. salt
- ½ tsp. finely ground pepper
- ⅓ cup dry sherry
- ½ tsp. Worcestershire sauce

garnishes

Fresh flat-leaf parsley, ground red pepper

1. Prepare Shrimp Stock: Peel shrimp, reserving shells. Cover and chill shrimp. Place shrimp shells, broth, next 6 ingredients, and 3 cups water in a large Dutch oven; bring to a boil over high heat. Cover, reduce heat to low, and simmer 45 minutes. Remove from heat. Pour through a fine wire-mesh strainer into a bowl, using back of a spoon to press out liquid. Discard solids. (Stock can be made up to 1 day ahead. Store in an airtight container in refrigerator.)
2. Prepare Bisque: Drain chilled shrimp well. Melt butter in a Dutch oven over medium-high heat. Add shrimp, and sauté 6 to 7 minutes or just until shrimp turn pink. Transfer shrimp to a plate or bowl using a slotted spoon. Reserve 8 shrimp. Add onion and next 2 ingredients to Dutch oven; sauté 6 to 8 minutes or until tender. Add 3¾ cups shrimp stock, wine, and next 2 ingredients. Bring to a boil; cover, reduce heat to low, and simmer 20 minutes.
3. Add cream and milk. Bring to a very gentle simmer over medium heat, stirring occasionally. Reduce heat to low, and cook 15 minutes or until thickened. Add salt, black pepper, and shrimp (all but the 8 reserved). Remove from heat, and process with a handheld blender until smooth.
4. Return Dutch oven to heat, just long enough to warm bisque, about 3 minutes. Stir in sherry and Worcestershire sauce. Ladle into 8 bowls or cups. Top each serving with 1 reserved shrimp. Garnish, if desired.

Makes: about 8 cups Hands-on Time: 45 min. Total Time: 2 hr., 25 min.

chicken and rolling pin dumplings

When I was in the hospital the night after my first child was born, my sister and dad brought me a steaming bowl of chicken and dumplings. With our brand-new baby beside me, it was one of the greatest meals of my life. Unlike the rounder lumps you find up North, soup dumplings in the South are usually flat strips. Get your rolling pin ready.

chicken and broth

- 1 (4-lb.) whole chicken
- 2 medium-size yellow onions, chopped
- 3 carrots, cut into ½-inch pieces
- 4 celery ribs, cut into ½-inch pieces
- 10 fresh parsley sprigs
- 2 bay leaves
- ½ tsp. black peppercorns

dumplings

- 3 cups self-rising soft-wheat flour (such as White Lily), plus more for the countertop
- 1½ tsp. salt
- ½ tsp. dried basil
- ½ tsp. freshly ground pepper
- ¼ tsp. ground thyme
- 6 Tbsp. shortening
- 1 cup milk

remaining ingredients

- ¾ tsp. salt
- ¾ tsp. freshly ground pepper

garnishes

chopped fresh dill, chopped fresh parsley

1. Prepare Chicken and Broth: Remove giblets and neck from chicken; reserve for another use. Place chicken, breast side up, and next 6 ingredients in a large Dutch oven. Cover with 16 cups water. Bring to a boil over high heat; cover, reduce heat to low, and simmer 1 hour or until chicken is done.

2. Remove chicken from Dutch oven; continue to simmer broth, uncovered, 45 minutes. Meanwhile, let chicken cool slightly. Remove and discard skin and bones. Shred meat.

3. Pour broth through a fine wire-mesh strainer into a large bowl; discard solids. Skim fat off surface, or use a fat separator to remove fat. Return 12 cups broth to Dutch oven, and bring to a boil over high heat. (Save remaining broth for another use.) Add shredded chicken; return to a boil while you make the dumplings.

4. Prepare Dumplings: Combine 3 cups flour and next 4 ingredients. Cut in shortening with a pastry blender or fork until crumbly. Add milk, stirring just until dry ingredients are moistened. Turn dough out onto a well-floured surface; knead dough 3 to 4 times or until smooth. Roll to ⅛-inch thickness. Cut into 1-inch-wide strips (about 3 inches long).

5. Drop strips, a few at a time, into boiling liquid. (Don't worry, they will all fit in the Dutch oven. Just keep gently nudging them to the side with a spoon and adding more. They'll look waterlogged and gooey and will thicken the broth beautifully.) Stir gently just once. Cover, reduce heat to medium, and simmer 30 minutes. Add ¾ tsp. each salt and pepper just before serving. Garnish, if desired.

Makes: 15 cups **Hands-on Time:** 45 min. **Total Time:** 4 hr.

sweet and smoky grilled brunswick stew

Grilling the pork and chicken gives this Southern classic a nice smoky flavor. Adding ground beef makes it even heartier—perfect to feed a crowd. If grilling doesn't fit your schedule, use 1½ lb. chopped roasted or rotisserie chicken and 2 lb. of your favorite chopped barbecued pork instead. I like to freeze any leftovers in single servings—ideal for a warm lunch on a busy day.

- 1 tsp. salt
- 1 tsp. freshly ground pepper
- 1 tsp. paprika
- 1 (4-lb.) whole chicken
- 1 (4-lb.) bone-in pork shoulder roast (Boston butt)
- ½ cup finely chopped yellow onion
- 1 Tbsp. minced garlic
- 1 Tbsp. vegetable oil
- 3 (15-oz.) cans tomato sauce
- ¾ cup sorghum syrup
- ½ cup cider vinegar
- ⅓ cup yellow mustard
- ¼ cup tomato paste
- ¼ cup Worcestershire sauce
- 3 Tbsp. light brown sugar
- 1 tsp. freshly ground pepper
- 2 tsp. hot sauce (such as Tabasco), plus more to taste
- 1 tsp. lemon zest
- 2 Tbsp. fresh lemon juice (about 1 lemon)
- 1 lb. lean ground beef
- 4 ears fresh corn
- 2 cups chicken broth
- 2 (28-oz.) cans crushed tomatoes
- 1 (10-oz.) package frozen English peas

1. Stir together first 3 ingredients. Cut chicken, using kitchen shears, along both sides of backbone, separating the backbone from the chicken. Remove and discard backbone. Sprinkle chicken and pork with salt mixture; rub seasoning into meat. Cover and chill chicken.

2. Preheat grill to 350° to 400° (medium-high) heat. Grill pork, fat side up, 1 hour and 30 minutes. Place chicken, breast side up, on grill with pork. Grill chicken, turning every 15 minutes, and pork 1 hour or until a meat thermometer registers 165° in thickest part of chicken thigh and 145° in pork.

3. Meanwhile, cook onion and garlic in hot oil in a very large Dutch oven over medium heat, stirring often, 5 minutes or until tender. Add tomato sauce and next 10 ingredients; stir until well blended. Reduce heat to low; cook, stirring occasionally, 20 minutes or until sauce is thickened and bubbly. Keep warm.

4. Brown ground beef in a large skillet over medium heat, stirring often, 10 minutes or until meat crumbles and is no longer pink; drain. Stir beef into tomato mixture. Cut corn from cobs, and place in a bowl, scraping milk and any remaining pulp from cobs. Add corn and liquid to tomato mixture.

5. Remove chicken and pork from grill; let stand 20 minutes. Chop chicken and pork, removing and discarding bones, skin, and fat. Add chicken, pork, broth, and crushed tomatoes to tomato mixture, and stir until blended.

6. Bring to a boil over low heat, stirring often (about 30 minutes). Simmer uncovered, stirring often, 1 hour and 25 minutes. Stir in peas, and cook 5 minutes. Add hot sauce to taste. Serve immediately.

Makes: about 6 qt. Hands-on Time: 1 hr., 20 min. Total Time: 5 hr., 5 min.

fried green tomato sandwiches

There have been summer mornings when, even before my first cup of coffee, I've set my sights on a sandwich of fried green tomatoes for lunch. With crispy cornmeal-crusted tomato slices, bacon, and herbed mayonnaise, the midday meal doesn't get much better than this.

½ cup mayonnaise
2 Tbsp. minced fresh chives
1 Tbsp. chopped fresh basil
1 Tbsp. chopped fresh oregano
½ tsp. salt
½ tsp. freshly ground pepper
4 onion rolls, split and toasted
4 Bibb lettuce leaves
4 to 8 (½-inch-thick) slices Fried Green Tomatoes (page 55)
8 cooked bacon slices

1. Combine first 6 ingredients in a small bowl.
2. Spread herbed mayonnaise over cut sides of rolls. Layer lettuce leaves, tomato slices, and bacon on bottom halves of rolls. Cover with top halves of rolls.

Makes: 4 servings Hands-on Time: 10 min.
Total Time: 10 min., not including Fried Green Tomatoes

grilled cheese and tomato sandwiches

(pictured on facing page, top)

If you like grilled cheese sandwiches with tomato soup, my version is a two-in-one. I brown thick tomato slices and layer them between the cheeses before grilling the sandwiches.

1 large tomato
2 Tbsp. extra virgin olive oil
¼ tsp. salt
¼ tsp. freshly ground pepper
2 to 3 Tbsp. butter, softened
8 multigrain bread slices
Wax paper
2 oz. Havarti cheese, shredded (½ cup)
2 oz. sharp Cheddar cheese, shredded (½ cup)

1. Peel tomato with a vegetable peeler, trim and discard the end pieces, and cut the remainder into 4 thick slices. Rub slices with olive oil, and sprinkle with salt and pepper. Cook tomato slices in a large nonstick skillet over medium heat 1 to 2 minutes on each side or until browned. (Turn tomatoes only once, being careful not to tear.)
2. Spread butter on 1 side of each bread slice. Place 4 bread slices, buttered sides down, on wax paper. Top each evenly with Havarti cheese, grilled tomato slices, and Cheddar cheese. Top with remaining bread slices, buttered sides up.
3. Cook sandwiches in a large skillet or griddle over medium heat, gently pressing with a spatula, 2 to 3 minutes on each side or until sandwiches are golden brown and cheeses are melted.
Makes: 4 servings   Hands-on Time: 20 min.   Total Time: 20 min.

fried oyster po'boys (pictured on page 187, bottom right)

Serve these big sandwiches for a filling lunch or casual supper. If oysters aren't on hand, these are just as good with fried shrimp.

4 small French bread loaves
Vegetable oil
1 cup mayonnaise
1 Tbsp. chopped fresh flat-leaf parsley
2 Tbsp. finely chopped shallots
2 Tbsp. tomato paste
1½ Tbsp. sweet-hot pickle relish
1 Tbsp. fresh lemon juice
⅛ tsp. hot sauce
1 sleeve saltine crackers, finely crushed
¾ tsp. salt
¾ tsp. freshly ground pepper
1 cup buttermilk
1 large egg
1 pt. fresh standard oysters, drained
Shredded iceberg lettuce

1. Preheat oven to 200°. Place a wire rack on a baking sheet, and place in oven. Split bread loaves lengthwise, and scoop out most of centers. Reserve for another use. Place hollowed-out loaves on wire rack in oven, and warm 20 minutes (until you're ready to assemble the sandwiches).
2. Meanwhile, pour vegetable oil to depth of 1 inch in a large Dutch oven; heat to 375°.
3. Combine mayonnaise and next 6 ingredients in a bowl. Combine crackers, salt, and pepper in a second bowl. Whisk together buttermilk and egg in a third bowl.
4. Dip oysters in buttermilk mixture; dredge in cracker crumbs. Fry in hot oil, in 2 batches, 1 to 2 minutes or until golden brown. Drain on a wire rack over paper towels.
5. Remove bread from oven. Spread cut sides of loaves with mayonnaise mixture; fill with oysters and shredded lettuce.
Makes: 4 servings Hands-on Time: 35 min. Total Time: 35 min.

ham salad croissants (pictured on page 187, bottom left)

I enjoyed ham salad growing up and still find it a perfect way to reinvent ham left over from big holiday dinners. If no holiday ham is in sight, buy an unsliced pound of ham from the deli counter.

1 lb. cooked ham
½ cup mayonnaise
½ cup diced Vidalia onion
¼ cup diced red bell pepper
1½ Tbsp. dill pickle relish
2 tsp. seeded and diced jalapeño pepper
1 tsp. fresh lemon juice
½ tsp. Dijon mustard
12 miniature croissants
4 green leaf lettuce leaves
Garnish: dill pickle chips

1. Cut ham into large cubes. Pulse in a food processor 12 times or until minced. Transfer to a medium bowl. Add mayonnaise and next 6 ingredients. Stir until blended.
2. Slice croissants nearly in half horizontally (cutting to, but not through, other side). Tear each lettuce leaf into three pieces. Divide lettuce pieces and ham salad evenly among croissants. Garnish, if desired.
Makes: 12 servings Hands-on Time: 20 min. Total Time: 20 min.

**table talk:
children's table**
What big Southern gathering or holiday meal is complete without a special table for the little ones? A miniature table with smaller chairs makes meals more comfortable for the children, who are usually thrilled to be dining without their parents at their elbows.

These tiny tables range from modern and easy-to-clean plastic styles to beautiful antique hardwood designs complete with leaves. Some newer folding card tables even lower to a level ideal for kids. The table shown here has been in my family for generations. It's quite popular for meals, intense coloring sessions, and tea parties with hungry baby dolls.

catfish sandwiches with corn relish

Family fish fries are a Southern Friday-night tradition. Soft hoagie rolls and colorful relish turn the signature fried fish of the South into unique and pretty sandwiches.

Vegetable oil
2 catfish fillets (about 13 oz.)
¼ tsp. salt
¼ tsp. freshly ground pepper
½ cup plain yellow cornmeal
½ cup all-purpose flour
1 cup buttermilk
1 large egg
8 leaves Bibb or green leaf lettuce
8 split-top hoagie rolls
2 cups Corn Relish

1. Pour oil to depth of 3 inches in a Dutch oven over medium heat; heat to 375°.
2. Cut catfish lengthwise into 4 strips each. Sprinkle with salt and pepper. Combine cornmeal and flour in a shallow bowl. Combine buttermilk and egg in a second shallow bowl.
3. Dredge fish in flour mixture, dip in buttermilk mixture, and dredge in flour mixture again. Fry fish, in batches, in hot oil, turning once, 3 minutes or until cornmeal coating is golden brown and fish flakes with a fork. Drain on a wire rack over paper towels.
4. Place lettuce on bottom half of rolls. Divide fish among rolls. Top with Corn Relish (about ¼ cup each) and roll tops.
Makes: 8 servings Hands-on Time: 30 min.
Total Time: 40 min., including relish

corn relish

2 cups fresh corn kernels (4 ears)
½ cup diced red onion
½ cup diced red bell pepper
¼ cup cider vinegar
1 Tbsp. chopped fresh parsley
1 Tbsp. light brown sugar
1 jarred pepperoncini salad pepper, sliced
1 Tbsp. liquid from pepperoncini salad pepper jar

1. Stir together all ingredients in a bowl. Cover and chill until ready to serve.
Makes: 3¼ cups Hands-on Time: 10 min. Total Time: 10 min.

kentucky hot brown sandwiches

Chef Fred Schmidt at The Brown Hotel in Louisville, Kentucky, designed an open-faced sandwich elegant enough for company and filling enough for a cold winter supper. It was first created in the 1920s to feed guests hungry after a night of dancing. Traditionally made with turkey, it's a great use of leftovers from the holiday bird. Shredded roasted or rotisserie chicken makes a good substitute.

2 Tbsp. unsalted butter
2½ Tbsp. all-purpose flour
2 cups milk
5 oz. white Cheddar cheese, shredded (1¼ cups)
½ tsp. salt
¼ tsp. freshly ground pepper
4 (¾-inch-thick) bakery bread slices, toasted
1 tomato, cut into 8 (¼-inch-thick) slices
1 lb. pulled roasted turkey or chicken (about 3 cups)
½ cup freshly grated Parmigiano-Reggiano cheese
8 cooked bacon slices

1. Preheat broiler with oven rack 5 inches from heat. Melt butter in a heavy saucepan over low heat; whisk in flour until smooth. Cook 1 minute, whisking constantly. Gradually whisk in milk. Cook mixture over medium heat, whisking constantly, until it is thickened and bubbly (about 15 minutes). Remove from heat; add Cheddar cheese and next 2 ingredients, stirring until cheese is melted.
2. Place 1 bread slice in each of 4 gratin dishes or ovenproof plates. Top each with 2 tomato slices. Top with turkey, cheese sauce, and Parmigiano-Reggiano cheese.
3. Broil 3 minutes or until lightly browned and bubbly. Top each sandwich with 2 bacon slices, crisscrossing slices. Serve immediately.

Makes: 4 servings   Hands-on Time: 30 min.   Total Time: 35 min.

pimiento cheese-stuffed burgers

I would be one happy woman if I had a little pimiento cheese at every meal. Finding God's greatest spread inside a juicy hamburger is a welcome surprise.

3 oz. sharp Cheddar cheese
1 (2-oz.) jar diced pimiento, drained
1 oz. cream cheese, softened
1 Tbsp. mayonnaise
2 lb. ground chuck
½ tsp. salt
¼ tsp. freshly ground pepper
6 hamburger buns, toasted
Green leaf lettuce leaves, sliced tomato, dill pickle chips, and sliced red onion

1. Preheat grill to 350° to 400° (medium-high) heat. Grate Cheddar cheese on the large holes of a box grater. Place cheese in a large bowl. Add pimiento, cream cheese, and mayonnaise, stirring until well blended.
2. Divide ground chuck into 6 equal portions. Shape each portion into a ball. Poke a large hole in center of each ball using your index finger. Fill each hole with 2 Tbsp. pimiento cheese. Mold meat around cheese, completely enclosing cheese. Flatten to ¾-inch-thick patties, being careful not to open cheese-stuffed holes. Sprinkle with salt and pepper.
3. Grill, covered with grill lid, 6 minutes on each side or until beef is no longer pink. Let stand 5 minutes. Serve burgers on buns with lettuce, tomato, pickles, and onion.
Makes: 6 servings Hands-on Time: 25 min. Total Time: 30 min.

double BLTs

For a new twist on the Southern lunchtime favorite, turn your BLT into a double-decker. Top-quality bacon and heirloom tomatoes make it a real luxury high-rise.

4 thick-cut bacon slices (about ½ lb.)
1 large onion, cut into ½-inch-thick slices
12 thin sourdough bread slices
⅔ cup mayonnaise
2 lb. tomatoes, sliced
4 green leaf lettuce leaves
Wooden picks

1. Cook bacon in a large skillet over medium-low heat 12 minutes or until crisp. Remove bacon, and drain on paper towels, reserving drippings in skillet. Cut each slice in half crosswise.
2. Cook onion slices in hot drippings over medium heat 4 minutes on each side or until browned.
3. Spread 1 side of each bread slice with mayonnaise. Layer 4 bread slices, mayonnaise sides up evenly, with half of tomato slices and all of bacon. Top with 4 bread slices, mayonnaise sides up; layer with lettuce, onion, and remaining half of tomato slices. Top with remaining 4 bread slices, mayonnaise sides down. Secure with wooden picks, and cut in half.
Makes: 4 servings Hands-on Time: 30 min. Total Time: 30 min.

open-faced meatloaf sandwiches

On nights when I'm lucky enough to have a few slices of meatloaf left over, I know a hearty, comforting lunch is in my future. Meatloaf smothered in broiled cheese really hits the spot on chilly winter days.

4 thick slices Stuffed Meatloaf (page 120)
1 green onion, chopped, plus more for garnish
1 large tomato, sliced
4 slices provolone cheese
2 Tbsp. whole grain mustard
4 thick white bread slices, toasted (such as Pepperidge Farm Hearty white bread)
4 green leaf lettuce leaves

1. Preheat broiler with oven rack 4 inches from heat.
2. Arrange meatloaf slices in a jelly-roll pan. Top meatloaf with green onion, tomato slices, and cheese. Broil 2 minutes or until cheese melts and begins to brown.
3. Spread mustard on 1 side of each bread slice. Top with lettuce and meatloaf. Garnish, if desired. Serve immediately.

Makes: 4 servings Hands-on Time: 10 min.
Total Time: 12 min., not including meatloaf

my southern table

Growing up in southern Louisiana, Fridays were my favorite day of the week. My dad's side of the family all lived in their own homes on one huge piece of farmland, and we all came together, across this wide expanse of acreage, on Fridays.

The women in the family would gather at my mom's beauty shop, on one side of the house I grew up in, for some quality time together while they got their hair done. My grandmother was always first in line. That way, she could slip back to her house to prepare a lunch that kept our family nourished for the seven days to come.

Mom Landry, as we called her, was a gifted cook and a master at timing. She always remembered to put her meat on to marinate before she got her hair done. By the time all the ladies were looking beautiful and the men were meandering over to her house, lunch for 10 or more was hot and ready. We were starving for her cooking, and she always served real comfort food like steak and rice, fresh vegetables, and all the Southern sides.

The best part of these special days was that we were all together. As children, we would eat first and race off to play while the adults made their plates. Those are the afternoons that I'll always remember. It was that one small table in her house surrounded by so much farmland that was the gathering place for us all.

Now living in California, I miss those moments with everyone around the table. Thanks to my mom shipping me Cajun ingredients like crawfish and boudin, I can sometimes cook the food I was raised on. These meals at my own table are a reflection of home and a time when family and food were seamlessly connected.

Ali Landry
Model, actress, former Miss Louisiana and Miss USA
Cohost, TV Guide Network's *Hollywood Girls Night*

LOUISIANA
Walker & Sons
Mama's Shrimp Dip
CERTIFIED CAJUN
EVANGELINE PARISH, LOUISIANA
Home of the Cotton, Smoked Meat, Gumbo, Boggy Bayou, Swine & Cajun Music Festivals.
Visit Chicot State Park and the Crooked Creek Recreational Area. Come experience the wonderful people of Evangeline Parish, LA.
Walker & Sons

harvest time

salads, sides, and good things from the garden

english pea and radish salad (pictured on page 200, bottom left)

Finding fresh English peas can be tricky, so I created this salad with frozen peas. It's light, refreshing, and absolutely beautiful for a spring picnic. Use a mandoline or V-blade slicer to slice the radishes quickly and easily. A very brief blanching helps the peas retain their brilliant green color.

1 (16-oz.) package frozen petite green peas
1 cup very thinly sliced radishes
2 green onions, sliced (¼ cup)
2 Tbsp. chopped fresh mint, plus a few sprigs for garnish
2 Tbsp. extra virgin olive oil
2 Tbsp. fresh lemon juice
1 Tbsp. white wine vinegar
¾ tsp. salt
¼ tsp. freshly ground pepper

1. Fill a large bowl halfway with water and ice. Bring a medium saucepan filled with water to a boil. Add frozen peas, and cook 1 minute; drain. Plunge into ice water to stop the cooking process; drain. Combine peas and next 3 ingredients in a bowl.
2. Whisk together olive oil and next 4 ingredients until well blended. Pour over peas; toss to coat. Let stand 15 minutes before serving. Garnish, if desired.
Makes: 8 servings Hands-on Time: 10 min. Total Time: 30 min.

cucumber and tomato salad (pictured on page 200, right)

I've been making this salad for big Lang family gatherings for years, tweaking the recipe a little each time and using whatever tomatoes are at their peak. It's packed with flavor, and the bright colors liven up any buffet table.

3 Tbsp. red wine vinegar
2 Tbsp. extra virgin olive oil
1 Tbsp. honey
½ tsp. salt
½ tsp. freshly ground pepper
½ tsp. Dijon mustard
4 cups peeled and sliced English cucumber
1 Vidalia onion, quartered and thinly sliced
1 pt. grape tomatoes, cut in half
2 Tbsp. chopped fresh parsley

1. Whisk together first 6 ingredients in a large bowl. Add cucumber and remaining ingredients, and stir until blended. Cover and chill 1 hour. Serve with a slotted spoon.
Makes: 6 to 8 servings Hands-on Time: 20 min. Total Time: 1 hr., 20 min.

spicy coleslaw (pictured on page 200, top left)

This slaw is the best of three worlds: spicy, creamy, and crunchy. The buttermilk dressing rounds out the peppery bite of horseradish and jalapeño. Serve it as a side dish at fish fries, barbecues, and cookouts.

½ cup mayonnaise
¼ cup buttermilk
1 Tbsp. sugar
3 Tbsp. refrigerated extra-hot horseradish
2 Tbsp. cider vinegar
2 tsp. fresh lemon juice
1 to 2 tsp. hot sauce
½ tsp. salt
½ tsp. celery seeds
½ tsp. freshly ground black pepper
¼ tsp. dry mustard
4 cups finely chopped green cabbage
2 cups finely chopped red cabbage
1 cup shredded carrot
½ cup chopped red onion
3 green onions, thinly sliced
1 Tbsp. seeded and chopped jalapeño pepper

1. Whisk together first 11 ingredients in a small bowl until well blended.
2. Combine green cabbage and next 5 ingredients in a large bowl. Add mayonnaise mixture, and stir until well blended. Adjust seasonings to taste. Cover and chill 1 hour before serving.

Makes: 12 servings   Hands-on Time: 30 min.   Total Time: 1 hr., 30 min.

table talk:
farm table

Built with functionality in mind, farm tables met the many needs of early Americans, from enjoying meals to reading by candlelight. With simple legs and unadorned tops often made of one huge board, farm tables are extremely basic and beautiful pieces of furniture. Instead of chairs, many of these rustic tables have benches for seating.

Farm tables have gained popularity in recent years. The wonderful antique tables are highly prized for their character and charm. Many furniture companies make new versions in almost any size and finish.

heirloom tomato salad

Heirloom tomatoes are grown from seeds that have been saved from year to year. Their flavor is worlds away from the sort typically found in the produce department. The colors and shapes can vary greatly from one variety to another. So can the flavor. Choose several different kinds to create the prettiest summer salad. Taste and adjust the vinegar, salt, and pepper amounts to best highlight your unique tomatoes.

1½ lb. assorted heirloom tomatoes
¼ cup extra virgin olive oil
2 Tbsp. thinly sliced fresh basil, plus a few leaves for garnish
1½ Tbsp. red wine vinegar
¾ tsp. Dijon mustard
¼ tsp. flaked sea salt
⅛ tsp. freshly ground pepper

1. Cut tomatoes into ⅓-inch-thick slices. Arrange on a large serving plate.
2. Whisk together olive oil and next 5 ingredients in a 2-cup measuring cup. Pour olive oil mixture over tomato slices. Garnish, if desired.

Makes: 4 servings Hands-on Time: 10 min. Total Time: 10 min.

beet and chèvre salad

Beets are often overlooked and downplayed. Not in our house. We love them. I like to roast them and let their vibrant color and sweet, earthy flavor star in this pretty salad. To avoid staining your hands, slip on a pair of plastic or rubber gloves before you peel and cut the beets.

salad

⅔ cup chopped walnuts
4 lb. beets
2 Tbsp. extra virgin olive oil
1 tsp. salt
½ tsp. freshly ground pepper
2 oz. goat cheese, crumbled
½ cup sliced green onions

dressing

½ tsp. orange zest
2 Tbsp. fresh orange juice
2 tsp. extra virgin olive oil
¼ tsp. fresh thyme leaves, plus more for garnish
¼ tsp. salt
⅛ tsp. freshly ground pepper

1. Prepare Salad: Preheat oven to 350°. Bake walnuts in a single layer in a shallow pan 8 to 10 minutes or until toasted and fragrant, stirring halfway through. Remove from oven. Increase oven temperature to 400°.
2. Cut tops off beets. Gently wash beets, and peel. Cut beets into sixths. Toss with olive oil. Arrange in a jelly-roll pan. Sprinkle with salt and pepper.
3. Bake at 400° for 1 hour and 20 minutes or until fork-tender, stirring twice. Cool completely (about 30 minutes).
4. Arrange beets on a small serving platter. Top with walnuts, goat cheese, and green onions.
5. Prepare Dressing: Whisk together orange zest and next 5 ingredients. Drizzle over beet mixture. Garnish, if desired.
Makes: 4 to 6 servings Hands-on Time: 15 min.
Total Time: 2 hr., 15 min.

new potato salad with dill

New potatoes have tender red skins and wonderful flavor when boiled and tossed warm with a vinaigrette and fresh dill. Without the typical mayonnaise-based dressing, this lively potato salad is my go-to choice for picnics and tailgates.

- 1½ lb. new potatoes (about 10)
- 1 tsp. salt, divided
- 2 Tbsp. red wine vinegar
- 1 garlic clove, minced
- 1½ tsp. fresh lemon juice
- ½ tsp. Dijon mustard
- ¼ tsp. freshly ground pepper
- ¼ cup extra virgin olive oil
- 2 Tbsp. chopped fresh dill

1. Cut any potatoes larger than 2 inches in half. Bring potatoes, ½ tsp. salt, and 6 cups water to a boil in a large saucepan. Boil 10 minutes or until tender.
2. Meanwhile, whisk together vinegar, next 4 ingredients, and remaining ½ tsp. salt. Add olive oil in a slow, steady stream, whisking constantly until blended and smooth.
3. Drain potatoes, and place in a large serving bowl. Add vinaigrette to warm potatoes, and toss gently, being careful not to tear potatoes. Gently stir in dill. Serve warm or at room temperature.

Makes: 6 servings   Hands-on Time: 10 min.   Total Time: 35 min.

carolina gold rice salad

The golden color of a field of Carolina Gold rice is breathtaking to behold. The cherished long-grain rice almost disappeared after the Great Depression. It is now being farmed again near Charleston, South Carolina, and in several other states. In this salad, the rice soaks up a citrusy dressing. It tastes even better the next day.

- ½ cup pine nuts
- 1½ cups uncooked Carolina Gold long-grain rice
- 1 tsp. lemon zest
- ¼ cup fresh lemon juice (about 2 lemons)
- 2 Tbsp. fresh orange juice
- 2 Tbsp. white balsamic vinegar
- ¾ tsp. salt
- ⅛ tsp. freshly ground pepper
- 2 Tbsp. extra virgin olive oil
- 1 cup sliced green onions
- ⅓ cup golden raisins

1. Cook pine nuts in a skillet over medium-low heat, stirring often, 5 minutes or until toasted and fragrant.
2. Cook rice according to package directions. (You should have about 6 cups.)
3. Whisk together lemon zest and next 5 ingredients. Add olive oil in a slow, steady stream, whisking until blended and smooth.
4. Combine hot cooked rice, green onions, raisins, and pine nuts. Pour dressing over rice mixture, and stir until blended. Let stand 30 minutes before serving, or cover, chill, and serve the next day.

Makes: 6 servings   Hands-on Time: 15 min.   Total Time: 55 min.

Note: Carolina Gold rice can be found at specialty grocery stores across the South. If you can't find it in your area, you can purchase it online at boiledpeanuts.com, foodforthesouthernsoul.com, ansonmills.com, or substitute regular long-grain rice.

roasted chicken salad

Roasting your own chicken makes this chicken salad divine. Combining the ingredients while the chicken is still warm allows the flavors to marry. If you're lucky enough to find yellow or orange cherry tomatoes, try them for a burst of color.

1 (4-lb.) whole chicken
1 lemon, quartered
2 garlic cloves
¾ tsp. freshly ground pepper
1 tsp. salt, divided
2 tsp. extra virgin olive oil
¾ cup cherry tomatoes, cut in half
⅔ cup mayonnaise
2 Tbsp. diced red onion
1 Tbsp. chopped fresh flat-leaf parsley
Garnish: fresh basil
Poppy seed crackers

1. Preheat oven to 450°. If applicable, remove giblets from chicken, and reserve for another use. Place lemon and garlic in cavity. Loosen and lift skin from chicken breasts with fingers (do not totally detach skin); rub pepper and ½ tsp. salt underneath skin. Carefully replace skin. Rub skin with olive oil. Place chicken on a rack in a roasting pan.
2. Bake chicken at 450° for 25 minutes. Reduce oven temperature to 350°, and bake 1 hour or until a meat thermometer inserted into thickest portion of thigh registers 180°. Let stand 10 minutes.
3. Remove skin from chicken. Cut meat from bone. Shred into small strips, using 2 forks.
4. Combine chicken, tomato halves, next 3 ingredients, and remaining ½ tsp. salt. Cover and chill 1 hour. Garnish, if desired. Serve with poppy seed crackers.
Makes: 8 servings Hands-on Time: 20 min. Total Time: 2 hr., 55 min.

marinated asparagus and pecan salad

I love serving salads and vegetable sides on platters. They look pretty laid out, and it's more inviting than diving into a big bowl. This knife-and-fork salad is best made with pencil-thin asparagus. The green stalks should have just a hint of crunch after cooking.

¾ cup pecan halves
3 Tbsp. extra virgin olive oil
2 Tbsp. white wine vinegar
1 Tbsp. molasses
1 shallot, minced
½ tsp. salt
¼ tsp. freshly ground pepper
1 lb. very thin fresh asparagus spears
¼ cup crumbled blue cheese
Garnish: chopped tomato

1. Preheat oven to 350°. Bake pecan halves in a single layer in a shallow ovenproof pan 10 to 12 minutes or until toasted and fragrant, stirring halfway through. Cool slightly, and chop.
2. Combine olive oil and next 5 ingredients in a small bowl.
3. Snap off and discard tough ends of asparagus. Cook asparagus in boiling water to cover 2 minutes or until crisp-tender and bright green; drain. Plunge into ice water to stop the cooking process; drain. Toss asparagus immediately with oil mixture. Cover and refrigerate 30 minutes.
4. Remove asparagus from oil mixture, reserving oil mixture, and arrange on a platter. Top with pecans and cheese. Drizzle with reserved oil mixture. Garnish, if desired.
Makes: 6 servings Hands-on Time: 15 min. Total Time: 55 min.

old-fashioned collard greens

It's not uncommon for Southerners to "put on a pot of collards" at lunchtime and cook them until supper. When shopping for collard greens, buy by the bunch. Avoid bunches with shriveled and yellowed leaves.

1½ lb. smoked ham hocks
1 Tbsp. hot sauce (such as Tabasco)
1 tsp. celery salt
3 bunches fresh collard greens (about 2¾ lb.)
Hot Pepper Vinegar (page 225)

1. Place first 3 ingredients and 1 qt. water in a large Dutch oven. Bring to a boil; simmer, uncovered, 1 hour.
2. Trim and discard thick stems from bottom of collard green leaves. Tear leaves into 2-inch pieces. Place leaves in a large bowl of water. Swish leaves around to remove any dirt. Remove leaves from bowl, and discard water. Add leaves to Dutch oven; stir. (The pot will be full, but the leaves will cook down.) Cover and simmer, stirring every 30 minutes, for 1½ hours.
3. Remove ham hocks; remove meat from hocks, and chop. Discard any fat. Return meat to Dutch oven. Serve greens with a slotted spoon. Pass with Hot Pepper Vinegar. Reserve and enjoy potlikker.
Makes: 6 servings **Hands-on Time: 20 min.** **Total Time: 3 hr.**

Note: Potlikker is the liquid that remains in the pot after greens are cooked. It's packed with vitamins from the greens and is often enjoyed in a small soup bowl with cornbread. Some Southerners dunk cornbread in it; others crumble the bread right into the bowl. No matter the amount, it's *never* acceptable to throw out the potlikker.

swiss chard with bacon butter

While teaching a cooking class in Dallas, I learned a new term for bacon drippings. The very talented women in the kitchen with me called it "bacon butter." I was instantly intrigued. Whatever you call it, it's delicious on chard. Cooking the leaves briefly preserves their bright green color.

1 bunch Swiss chard (about 1 lb.)
1 Tbsp. bacon drippings
1 Tbsp. unsalted butter
½ tsp. freshly ground pepper
¼ tsp. salt

1. Remove chard leaves from stems by folding the leaves lengthwise so that the stem can be easily cut off. Cut leaves crosswise into ½-inch strips, and cut stems into ¾-inch pieces.
2. Heat bacon drippings and butter in a large skillet over medium heat. Add chard stems, and sauté 4 minutes. Add chard leaves, pepper, and salt, and sauté 4 minutes. Serve immediately.
Makes: 4 servings Hands-on Time: 25 min. Total Time: 25 min.

signature pieces: salt cellars and salt spoons
The practice of storing salt in cellars originated in Europe at a time when salt was considered a precious commodity. Old salt cellars are very small bowls with similarly petite spoons, often about 2 inches long. Cellars can range from extremely ornate porcelain to simple carved wood.

Older silver salt spoons were gilded to prevent corrosion. In recent years, salt spoons have evolved into more whimsical shapes, such as shells or leaves. Salt cellars still make appearances on Southern tables, mainly for very formal occasions. Pinching salt from the cellar generally is not considered good manners. The spoon should be used and returned to the cellar after each use.

roasted carrots, turnip roots, and vidalias

I have to think twice before I talk about turnips with my family. Dad calls the greens "turnips" and the roots "turnip roots." Mama calls the roots simply "turnips." No matter what you call them, roasting them brings out their natural sweetness.

2 lb. carrots
1 lb. turnip roots, cut into 1½-inch pieces (about 3 medium turnip roots)
1 lb. Vidalia onions, cut into 1½-inch pieces (about 1 large onion)
¼ cup extra virgin olive oil
1 tsp. salt
½ tsp. freshly ground pepper

1. Preheat oven to 450°.
2. Cut carrots in half lengthwise and, if they are large, into 4-inch pieces. Arrange carrots, turnip roots, and onion on 2 jelly-roll pans.
3. Toss vegetables with olive oil, and sprinkle with salt and pepper.
4. Bake at 450° for 55 minutes or until tender and beginning to brown, stirring vegetables and rotating pans once halfway through baking.
Makes: 6 servings Hands-on Time: 20 min. Total Time: 1 hr., 15 min.

creamed silver queen corn

Silver Queen is a variety of white corn with milky, creamy kernels. It's beloved for its lightly sweet flavor. Don't be tempted to just cut the corn from the cob with a knife. A corn cutter or creamer creates much, much creamier corn. I use the same wooden corn cutter that my grandmother Sa used. It's one of my prized possessions. Look for your own antique cutter at estate sales—or for brand-new ones made of wood or stainless steel at hardware and cookware stores. No matter the material, this Southern tool makes creamed corn like nothing else.

13 ears fresh corn, husks removed
1 cup milk
2 Tbsp. unsalted butter
½ tsp. salt
⅛ tsp. freshly ground pepper

1. Remove silks from corn. Use a corn cutter and creamer set over a bowl to cut and cream the kernels from the cobs.
2. Transfer creamed corn to a large skillet. Add milk and next 2 ingredients. Cook over low heat, stirring often, 30 minutes. (If corn becomes too thick, add more milk until desired consistency.) Sprinkle with pepper.
Makes: 6 to 8 servings Hands-on Time: 25 min. Total Time: 55 min.

whole fried okra

Be picky when picking out okra. Large pods can be tough and stringy. Small pods are much better for frying whole. As for cornmeal, use what you prefer. White cornmeal is prized in much of the South, but yellow lends a richer color to fried foods.

- 1 lb. fresh okra
- 2 cups buttermilk
- Vegetable oil
- 1 cup all-purpose flour
- 1 cup plain white or yellow cornmeal
- ½ tsp. salt
- ½ tsp. freshly ground pepper

1. Combine okra and buttermilk; chill 30 minutes.
2. Pour vegetable oil to depth of 1 inch in a Dutch oven. Heat to 350°.
3. Combine flour, cornmeal, salt, and pepper in a shallow bowl.
4. Drain okra, and dredge in flour mixture. Fry okra, in 4 batches, in hot oil 2 minutes or until golden and crispy.
5. Drain on a wire rack over paper towels. Sprinkle with additional salt and pepper to taste while still hot. Serve immediately.
Makes: 6 servings Hands-on Time: 20 min. Total Time: 50 min.

corn fritters with summer salsa

Fresh corn is best when cooked a day or two after it's picked. Make the salsa with vine-ripened tomatoes, and you'll have the season's finest all on one plate.

- 4 ears fresh corn, husks removed
- ¾ cup plain white or yellow cornmeal
- ½ cup milk
- ¼ cup self-rising flour
- 1 large egg
- ½ tsp. salt
- ¼ tsp. freshly ground pepper
- ¼ cup vegetable oil
- Summer Salsa

1. Cut kernels from cobs; discard cobs. (You should have about 2 cups kernels.)
2. Whisk together cornmeal and next 5 ingredients in a medium bowl. Stir in kernels.
3. Heat vegetable oil in a large nonstick skillet over medium-high heat.
4. Working in 4 batches, spoon heaping tablespoonfuls of batter into hot oil, and flatten gently. Fry 2 to 3 minutes on each side or until browned. Drain on a wire rack over paper towels. Top each fritter with 2 tsp. Summer Salsa.
Makes: 24 fritters Hands-on Time: 36 min.
Total Time: 46 min., including salsa

summer salsa

- 1 cup chopped tomato
- 2 Tbsp. diced green onions
- ½ tsp. seeded and diced jalapeño pepper
- 1 Tbsp. fresh lemon juice (about 1 lemon)
- 1 tsp. chopped fresh parsley
- 4 pitted kalamata olives, finely chopped
- ¼ tsp. salt

1. Stir together all ingredients until well blended.
Makes: 1¼ cups Hands-on Time: 10 min. Total Time: 10 min.

mimi's pink-eyed purple hull peas

My children call my mama "Mimi." She cooks peas throughout the summer for all of us. When Dad buys more bushels than we can eat, they both spend a few days putting up peas. Pink-eyed purple hull peas are shaped similar to black-eyed peas, but they have deep purple hulls and little pink eyes. Fresh, they are a Southern summer delicacy, and much better than those in the frozen food case.

1 lb. fresh pink-eyed purple hull peas, shelled (about 3 cups)
1 (8- to 10-oz.) smoked ham hock
1 tsp. salt
Hot Pepper Vinegar

1. Bring peas, ham hock, salt, and 5 cups water to a boil in a 4-qt. saucepan over medium heat. Reduce heat to low, and cook, partially covered, 45 minutes or until peas are tender.
2. Drain peas, and remove ham hock. Cut meat from ham hock, and return to peas, if desired. Discard bone. Season with salt and freshly ground pepper to taste. Pass with Hot Pepper Vinegar.
Makes: 6 servings Hands-on Time: 5 min.
Total Time: 1 hr., not including pepper sauce

hot pepper vinegar

I'm never without a bottle of hot pepper vinegar in the door of my fridge. We eat the pepper-infused vinegar on just about every kind of pea during the summer, and we douse greens with it in the winter. It can be purchased at some grocery stores, but homemade is always better. And it's so easy to make:

Cut small slits in the sides of fresh cayenne or tabasco peppers, and pack them loosely in a clean, sterilized glass bottle or jar. Pour enough boiling white vinegar over the peppers to cover them completely. Cool completely. Cover and store in refrigerator. Chill for 3 weeks before using. To make more when you run low, just add more boiling vinegar to the bottled peppers.

grilled summer squash with rosemary

On hot summer days, it's a bonus to cook our entire supper outdoors. I grill the squash first and the main dish while the squash cools. Rosemary, smoke, and a kiss of molasses turn these prolific summer vegetables into a terrific side dish.

- 1½ lb. yellow squash (5 medium)
- 1½ lb. zucchini (7 small)
- 2 Tbsp. chopped fresh rosemary, plus more for garnish
- 3 Tbsp. extra virgin olive oil
- 2 Tbsp. molasses
- 2 Tbsp. white wine vinegar
- 2 garlic cloves, minced
- 1 tsp. salt
- ¼ tsp. freshly ground pepper

1. Cut squash and zucchini lengthwise into ¼-inch-thick slices.
2. Combine rosemary and next 6 ingredients in a large zip-top plastic freezer bag. Add squash and zucchini; seal and let stand 30 minutes.
3. Preheat grill to 350° to 400° (medium-high) heat.
4. Remove squash and zucchini from marinade, reserving 2 Tbsp. marinade. Grill squash and zucchini, in 2 batches, covered with grill lid, 4 to 5 minutes on each side or until crisp-tender. Arrange squash and zucchini on a serving platter, and drizzle with reserved 2 Tbsp. marinade. Garnish, if desired.

Makes: 6 to 8 servings Hands-on Time: 30 min. Total Time: 1 hr.

lemon-and-cheese-stuffed squash blossoms

Fried squash blossoms were once known in the Deep South as "poor man's fish." (Once fried, they resemble what you find at a fish fry.) Today, they are nothing short of a delicacy. The blossoms have a very short shelf life and ideally should be cooked the day they are picked. Look for them at your local farmers' market.

- 4 oz. cream cheese, softened
- 4 oz. goat cheese
- 1 Tbsp. chopped fresh basil
- 1 tsp. lemon zest
- 1 egg yolk
- ¼ tsp. salt
- ⅛ tsp. freshly ground pepper
- Vegetable oil
- 12 squash blossoms, rinsed and gently patted dry
- 1⅓ cups all-purpose flour
- 1⅛ cups club soda
- ¼ tsp. salt

1. Combine first 7 ingredients in a medium bowl.
2. Pour vegetable oil to depth of 1 inch in a Dutch oven; heat to 400° over medium heat (about 25 minutes).
3. Meanwhile, transfer cream cheese mixture to a large zip-top plastic freezer bag. Snip 1 corner of bag to make a small hole.
4. Carefully cut out and discard pistils inside each blossom using kitchen shears. Trim squash blossom stems to 1 inch. Pipe cheese mixture into blossoms just to the point where the petals begin to form a star when opened, being careful not to overfill. Twist petals of each blossom together to seal. Chill 10 minutes.
5. Whisk together flour, club soda, and salt in a medium bowl.
6. Dip chilled blossoms into batter, shaking off excess. Fry blossoms, in 3 batches, 2 to 3 minutes or until lightly browned. Serve immediately.

Makes: 6 servings Hands-on Time: 30 min. Total Time: 40 min.

stuffed baked vidalias

The South's famous sweet onions are grown only around Vidalia, Georgia. The low pH of the soil gives the onions a mild, sweet, irresistible flavor. In onion country, we eat them nearly every way possible.

4 (12-oz.) Vidalia onions
¼ tsp. salt
⅛ tsp. freshly ground pepper
1 lb. ground pork sausage
4 oz. sharp Cheddar cheese, grated on the small holes of a box grater (about 1 cup)
1 Tbsp. Dijon mustard

1. Preheat oven to 350°. Cut ½ inch from top of each onion. Leaving root end intact, cut off a small amount of root to make a flat bottom. Hollow out center of each onion, leaving ¾-inch thickness on bottom and sides, using a grapefruit knife or paring knife. Reserve removed onion for another use.
2. Sprinkle onion cavities with salt and pepper. Arrange in an 8-inch square baking dish; cover with aluminum foil.
3. Bake at 350° for 1 hour or until fork-tender.
4. Preheat broiler with oven rack 8 inches from heat. Brown sausage in a medium skillet over medium heat, stirring often, 8 minutes or until meat crumbles and is no longer pink. Drain on and blot with paper towels.
5. Combine sausage, cheese, and mustard. Carefully spoon into cavities of hot onions, mounding sausage mixture on top of onions. Broil 2 to 3 minutes or until stuffing is browned and bubbly.
Makes: 4 main-dish or 8 side-dish servings Hands-on Time: 30 min.
Total Time: 1 hr., 35 min.

my southern table

I love a good dining room table—so much that I actually have three of them in my Atlanta home. I'm a sucker for having exactly the right atmosphere, so I've got one formal, one casual, and one that's in between.

All of the dining tables in my home mean something special to me. In the designated formal dining room, I have an English Regency-style reproduction table made of mahogany. The fine woodwork on this table and intricate detailing seem to make the food presented on it look better than it is—which is important since I'm not a good cook. This table gets used for important conferences and meetings and for truly significant dining occasions that call for the pomp and circumstance of a formal dining room.

In what has become the designated breakfast area sits a table that I purchased as a Christmas present for my mom with the first real paycheck I ever made. It's an Italian farm table. Although it's not really my personal style or what I would choose to purchase for myself, it means a great deal to me. My mom thought it would be a nice place for our family to gather when we were all home, so I bought it for her for Christmas despite her protests that it was too expensive. It has been six years since she passed away, and now my two children, Gavin and Vera, sit at the head of the table in side-by-side high chairs. It's a nice way of connecting Mom to two grandchildren that she never got to meet.

The last and final dining table sits at the end of an office addition completed just before my daughter was born. It is an Antonio Citterio table made of wenge, a tropical wood, and it was the first dining room table I ever bought for myself. I had coveted this table for so long after having placed it in a few client homes. The über-clean lines appealed to my architectural-minimalist side, while the warm chocolate wood with its incredible graining appealed to the side of me that thinks of my home as a warm nest. Now it is the site of casual conferences and meetings, gift wrapping, library research, and a welcome middle ground between the too-formal dining room and the too-casual breakfast room. My hope is that it will also be the future site of much of my children's homework.

Vern Yip

Interior designer and television design star

Host of HGTV's *Deserving Design;* judge, *HGTV Design Star*

www.unopiu.it
SW 6216 Jasper
SW 6215 Rocky River
SW 6214 Underseas
SW 6213 Halcyon Green
SW 6212 Quietude
WOOD TOP?

sugar bowls

desserts to satisfy a southern sweet tooth

berry napoleons with buttermilk whipped cream (pictured on page 232)

Buttermilk and lime zest add tang and zip to the cream in these scrumptious stacked pastries. It's good to remember that phyllo dough dries out very quickly. While working, keep unused sheets covered with plastic wrap and a damp towel.

5 frozen phyllo sheets, thawed
5 Tbsp. unsalted butter, melted
5 tsp. sugar
Parchment paper
2 cups assorted fresh berries (such as blackberries, blueberries, and sliced strawberries)
2½ Tbsp. sugar, divided
¼ tsp. lime zest
½ cup heavy cream
3 Tbsp. buttermilk
Garnish: fresh mint sprigs

1. Preheat oven to 350°. Unfold phyllo sheets on a flat work surface. Stack 5 phyllo sheets, brushing each sheet with 1 Tbsp. melted butter and sprinkling with 1 tsp. sugar. Cut into 12 squares, and transfer to a parchment paper-lined jelly-roll pan, spacing them about 1 inch apart.
2. Bake at 350° for 14 minutes or until golden brown and crispy.
3. Combine berries, 1 Tbsp. sugar, and lime zest.
4. Beat cream and buttermilk at high speed with an electric mixer until foamy; gradually add remaining 1½ Tbsp. sugar, beating until stiff peaks form.
5. Place 6 phyllo squares on individual serving plates; top each with 1½ Tbsp. whipped cream and 3 Tbsp. berry mixture. Top each with another phyllo square and equal portions of the remaining whipped cream and berries. Garnish, if desired, and serve immediately.
Makes: 6 servings   Hands-on Time: 25 min.   Total Time: 40 min.

blackberry one-biscuit mini cobblers

(pictured on page 233)

The fluffy, sugar-crusted biscuits on top are perfect for sopping up the tart, juicy berries on the bottom of these individual cobblers. Blackberries are sweetest in the summer and benefit from a little extra sugar at other times of the year. Taste and adjust the filling to suit your sweet tooth.

4 cups fresh blackberries
½ cup firmly packed light brown sugar (or more to taste)
1 tsp. lemon zest
1 tsp. vanilla extract
2 tsp. cornstarch
¼ tsp. salt
1 cup all-purpose soft-wheat flour (such as White Lily)
1 tsp. baking powder
½ tsp. salt
6 Tbsp. cold unsalted butter, cut into ½-inch cubes, plus more for buttering the dishes
½ cup plus 2 Tbsp. heavy cream
2 tsp. turbinado sugar
Garnish: fresh mint sprigs

1. Preheat oven to 350°. Combine blackberries and next 5 ingredients. Divide mixture among 4 (10-oz.) buttered ramekins. Place ramekins in an aluminum foil-lined jelly-roll pan. Bake 30 minutes.
2. Combine flour and next 2 ingredients. Cut butter into flour mixture with a pastry blender until mixture resembles small peas and dough is crumbly. Stir in cream just until dry ingredients are moistened, using your hands or a fork. Divide dough into 4 equal portions. Top ramekins with dough. Sprinkle with turbinado sugar.
3. Bake at 350° for 40 to 45 minutes or until lightly browned. Cool 30 minutes before serving. Garnish, if desired.
Makes: 4 servings   Hands-on Time: 20 min.   Total Time: 2 hr.

sorghum syrup rice pudding brûlée

Rice pudding is a gloriously creamy dessert—or breakfast, if you're so inclined. This version gets a crème brûlée-style torched sugar topping and highlights the unique flavor of sorghum syrup. Slathered on biscuits and sold at roadside farm stands throughout the South, sorghum syrup is as thick as honey and milder than molasses. If you can't find it in stores, try online at boiledpeanuts.com.

2½ cups milk
1 cup heavy cream
½ cup uncooked long-grain rice
¼ tsp. salt
2 egg yolks
3 Tbsp. sorghum syrup
1½ tsp. vanilla extract
½ tsp. ground cinnamon
½ cup sugar, divided
½ cup golden raisins

1. Bring first 4 ingredients to a boil in a 2-qt. heavy saucepan over medium heat, stirring constantly. Cover, reduce heat to low, and simmer, stirring occasionally, 15 minutes.
2. Whisk together egg yolks, next 3 ingredients, and ¼ cup sugar in a medium bowl. Gradually whisk 1 cup cream mixture into egg mixture. Whisk egg mixture into remaining cream mixture. Cook over low heat, stirring occasionally, 15 minutes or until pudding is thick and rice is tender. Add raisins; cook 1 minute.
3. Divide among 8 (6-oz.) ramekins. Place heavy-duty plastic wrap directly on warm pudding (to prevent a film from forming). Chill 4 to 18 hours.
4. Sprinkle remaining ¼ cup sugar onto pudding (about 1½ tsp. per ramekin). Carefully heat sugar until melted and caramelized using a kitchen torch. Let stand 1 minute before serving.
Makes: 8 servings Hands-on Time: 45 min. Total Time: 4 hr., 45 min.

real banana pudding

It's a simple, from-scratch dessert that often leaves me speechless: homemade vanilla pudding layered with vanilla wafer cookies and banana slices and topped with a cloud of meringue. Some like it warm. Others prefer it like I do: nice and cold. The hardest part is waiting for it to fully chill.

½ cup sugar
2 Tbsp. cornstarch
¼ tsp. salt
2¼ cups milk
4 large eggs, separated
2 Tbsp. unsalted butter
1 tsp. vanilla extract
3⅓ cups vanilla wafers
4 ripe bananas, cut into ⅓-inch-thick slices
3 Tbsp. sugar

1. Preheat oven to 375°. Whisk together first 3 ingredients in a small bowl. Whisk together sugar mixture, milk, and 4 egg yolks in a medium-size heavy saucepan until well blended. Cook over medium heat, stirring constantly, 6 to 8 minutes or until thickened. Remove from heat; stir in butter and vanilla.
2. Layer half of vanilla wafers in an 8-inch square baking dish. Top with half of banana slices and half of pudding. Repeat procedure with remaining wafers, banana slices, and pudding.
3. Beat egg whites at high speed with an electric mixer until foamy. Gradually add 3 Tbsp. sugar, beating until sugar dissolves and stiff peaks form. Spread meringue over pudding, sealing to edge of dish.
4. Bake at 375° for 7 to 10 minutes or until golden. Let cool 30 minutes, and serve warm; or chill an additional hour, and serve cold.
Makes: 8 to 10 servings Hands-on Time: 25 min.
Total Time: 1 hr., 5 min.

peach and blueberry cobbler

Cobbler cooked in a cast-iron skillet is as pretty as it is Southern. Pouring the simple batter into a hot skillet makes edges that are divinely crisp and chewy. If there's ever any left over from dessert, save it for breakfast the next morning.

½ cup unsalted butter
1 cup all-purpose flour
1 cup sugar
⅓ cup plain yellow cornmeal
1 Tbsp. baking powder
⅛ tsp. salt
1¼ cups milk
⅛ tsp. almond extract
2 cups fresh blueberries
2 cups peeled and thinly sliced fresh peaches (¼-inch-thick slices)

1. Preheat oven to 375°. Melt butter in a 10-inch cast-iron skillet in the oven as it preheats. Remove from oven when melted.
2. Whisk together flour and next 4 ingredients in a medium bowl. Add milk and almond extract, stirring just until dry ingredients are moistened.
3. Pour batter over melted butter in hot skillet. Sprinkle blueberries and peaches over batter.
4. Bake at 375° for 55 minutes or until golden brown. Serve warm.
Makes: 10 servings Hands-on Time: 15 min. Total Time: 1 hr., 10 min.

pound cake from heaven

In the South, we love a good pound cake. This one is positively heavenly—sweet and rich but still, somehow, light as a cloud.

1½ cups unsalted butter, softened
3 cups sugar
5 large eggs
3 cups all-purpose soft-wheat flour (such as White Lily)
1 tsp. baking powder
¼ tsp. salt
1 (5-oz.) can evaporated milk
⅔ cup heavy cream
1 Tbsp. vanilla extract
Garnishes: sweetened whipped cream, fresh strawberries

1. Preheat oven to 350°. Place butter in the bowl of a heavy-duty electric stand mixer, and beat at medium speed until light and fluffy (about 6 minutes). Gradually add sugar, beating until blended. Beat 1 minute more. Add eggs, 1 at a time, beating just until yellow disappears after each addition.
2. Combine flour and next 2 ingredients. Combine evaporated milk and cream; add to butter mixture alternately with flour mixture, beginning and ending with flour mixture. Beat at low speed just until blended after each addition, stopping to scrape bowl as needed. Stir in vanilla. Pour batter into a greased and floured 10-inch (16-cup) tube pan.
3. Bake at 350° for 1 hour and 15 minutes or until a long wooden pick inserted in center comes out clean. Cool in pan on a wire rack 1 hour; remove from pan to wire rack, and cool completely (about 1 hour). Garnish, if desired.
Makes: 12 servings   Hands-on Time: 15 min.   Total Time: 3 hr., 30 min.

six-layer caramel cake

On my birthday, I request one cake and one cake only. I can't turn a year older without a big slice (or two or three) of caramel cake. I didn't love it as a child, but at some point I came to my senses, and now it's something I crave. My theory is: the more layers, the better. Stack 'em high and dig in.

Vegetable cooking spray
Parchment paper
3 cups all-purpose soft-wheat flour (such as White Lily)
1 tsp. baking powder
½ tsp. salt
4 large eggs
1 cup milk
1½ tsp. vanilla extract
1 cup unsalted butter, softened
2 cups sugar
Caramel Frosting

1. Preheat oven to 350°. Coat 3 (9-inch) round cake pans with cooking spray. Line bottom of each pan with parchment paper; coat paper with cooking spray.
2. Whisk together flour, baking powder, and salt in a medium bowl. Whisk together eggs, milk, and vanilla in a second medium bowl.
3. Place butter and sugar in the bowl of a heavy-duty electric stand mixer, and beat at medium speed 3 minutes or until light and fluffy. Add flour mixture to butter mixture alternately with milk mixture, beginning and ending with flour mixture. Beat at low speed until blended after each addition. Increase speed to medium, and beat 2 minutes. (Batter will be thick.) Divide batter among prepared pans.
4. Bake at 350° for 23 to 25 minutes or until centers of cakes spring back when pressed lightly with your finger and a wooden pick inserted in center comes out clean. Cool in pans on wire racks 10 minutes. Remove from pans to wire racks; peel off and discard parchment paper, and cool completely (about 1 hour).
5. Wrap each layer in plastic wrap, and freeze 1 hour or until frozen solid. (Freezing the layers makes them easier to slice in half later.)
6. Remove plastic wrap from cake layers. Cut each cake layer in half horizontally using a long serrated knife. Let layers stand 30 minutes or until room temperature. (It is very important that the layers are not cold when frosting.)
7. Place 1 cake layer on a cake stand or serving plate. Working very quickly, spread a thin layer of frosting to edges. Repeat procedure with remaining cake layers and frosting. Spread remaining frosting on top and sides of cake. Let stand until frosting sets (about 1 hour).
Makes: 16 servings **Hands-on Time: 40 min.**
Total Time: 4 hr., 50 min., including frosting

caramel frosting

1 cup unsalted butter
2 cups firmly packed light brown sugar
½ tsp. salt
½ cup milk
4 cups powdered sugar, sifted
1 tsp. vanilla extract

1. Cook butter in a saucepan over low heat until melted. Stir in brown sugar and salt. Cook, stirring constantly, 2 minutes. Add milk, and bring to a boil, stirring constantly (about 6 minutes). Remove from heat. Let cool until warm, stirring occasionally (about 45 minutes).

2. Place sugar mixture in bowl of a heavy-duty electric stand mixer fitted with whisk attachment. Add powdered sugar, 1 cup at a time, beating at medium-low speed until blended after each addition, and scraping sides of bowl as needed. Add vanilla, and beat at medium speed 1 minute. Use immediately.

Makes: about 3 cups **Hands-on Time:** 20 min. **Total Time:** 1 hr., 5 min.

raspberry-lime coconut cake (pictured on page 232)

Coconut cakes simply don't get better than this. Raspberry jam and homemade lime curd take this cake beyond what you've tasted before. It's as pretty as it is delicious.

Vegetable cooking spray
Parchment paper
2 cups cake flour
2 tsp. baking powder
¼ tsp. salt
1 cup coconut milk
1½ tsp. vanilla extract
½ cup unsalted butter, softened
2 cups sugar
2 large eggs
2 egg whites
½ cup raspberry jam
3 cups unsweetened medium-to-large-flake coconut, toasted (such as Bob's Red Mill Unsweetened Flaked Coconut)
Lime Curd
Seven-Minute Coconut Frosting
Garnishes: fresh raspberries, lime slices

1. Preheat oven to 350°. Coat 3 (9-inch) round cake pans with cooking spray. Line bottom of each pan with parchment paper; coat paper with cooking spray.
2. Whisk together flour, baking powder, and salt in a medium bowl. Whisk together coconut milk and vanilla in a small bowl.
3. Beat butter and sugar at medium speed with an electric mixer until light and fluffy. Add eggs and egg whites, 1 at a time, beating well after each addition.
4. Add flour mixture to butter mixture alternately with coconut milk mixture, beginning and ending with flour mixture and stirring with a rubber spatula just until blended after each addition. (Do not overmix.) Divide batter among prepared cake pans.
5. Bake at 350° for 20 minutes or until centers of cakes spring back when pressed lightly with your finger and a wooden pick inserted in center comes out clean. Cool completely in pans on a wire rack (about 1 hour).
6. Remove from pans to wire racks; peel off and discard parchment paper. Cut any rounded tops off cake layers to make level tops using a serrated knife.
7. Heat raspberry jam in a small saucepan over low heat just until slightly melted (not hot).
8. Place 1 cake layer on a cake stand or serving plate. Spread raspberry jam over layer, covering completely. Sprinkle ½ cup coconut over jam. Top with 1 cake layer, and spread with Lime Curd, leaving a ½-inch border. Sprinkle ½ cup coconut over curd. Top with remaining cake layer, gently pressing to adhere. Spread top and sides of cake with Seven-Minute Coconut Frosting. Sprinkle with remaining toasted coconut. Garnish, if desired.
Makes: 12 servings Hands-on Time: 40 min.
Total Time: 5 hr., 35 min., including curd and frosting

lime curd

½ cup sugar
1 Tbsp. lime zest
¼ cup fresh lime juice (about 3 limes)
2 large eggs
5 Tbsp. unsalted butter, softened

1. Whisk together first 4 ingredients in a medium saucepan over medium-low heat. Cook, whisking constantly, until mixture just begins to thicken (about 5 minutes; do not boil). Remove from heat, and whisk in butter, 1 Tbsp. at a time, until well blended.
2. Transfer to a bowl, and place a piece of heavy-duty plastic wrap directly on warm curd (to prevent a film from forming). Chill 3 hours or until set. Curd can be made up to 1 day ahead.
Makes: 1¼ cups Hands-on Time: 15 min. Total Time: 3 hr., 15 min.

seven-minute coconut frosting

1 cup sugar
1 Tbsp. light corn syrup
3 egg whites
¼ tsp. cream of tartar
⅛ tsp. salt
¼ tsp. coconut extract

1. Pour water to depth of 1 inch in a small saucepan, and bring to a boil. Reduce heat to medium-low, and maintain at a simmer.
2. Whisk together first 5 ingredients and ⅓ cup water in a stainless-steel bowl. Place bowl over pan of simmering water, and beat sugar mixture in bowl at low speed with an electric mixer until blended. Increase speed to high, and beat until mixture is glossy and stiff peaks form (about 7 minutes).
3. Remove from heat. Add coconut extract; beat at high speed 1 to 2 minutes or until cooled slightly.
Makes: about 3 cups Hands-on Time: 15 min. Total Time: 20 min.

signature pieces:
silver flatware
Few items on the Southern table are more luxurious than sterling silver flatware. Patterns can be passed down for generations or selected new for a bride and groom. These precious metal pieces are often used only for formal dinners and holiday celebrations. Smooth and shiny, old or new, these eventual heirlooms are both personal and lavish.

Caring for sterling silver is more involved than looking after everyday stainless steel flatware. Silver needs to be polished when it's tarnished. The easiest way to minimize tarnish is to use the flatware often. The more it's used, the less often it needs polishing. For the best care, only hand wash sterling silver and remember to wash it separately from stainless steel.

hummingbird cake

Exactly how this cake got its name isn't clear, but it likely has to do with its flavor, sure to suit those nectar-loving hummingbirds and anyone with a love of dessert. The tropical fruit- and nut-studded cake first appeared in Southern Living *magazine in 1978. It's since become a signature cake of the South.*

1 cup chopped pecans
Vegetable cooking spray
Parchment paper
3 cups all-purpose soft-wheat flour (such as White Lily)
1½ cups sugar
1½ tsp. ground cinnamon
1 tsp. salt
1 tsp. baking soda
⅛ tsp. ground nutmeg
3 large eggs, lightly beaten
1½ cups vegetable oil
1½ tsp. vanilla extract
3 cups chopped bananas (about 4 medium bananas)
1 (8-oz.) can crushed pineapple in juice
Cream Cheese Frosting
Garnish: fresh thyme sprigs

1. Preheat oven to 350°. Bake pecans in a single layer in a shallow pan 6 to 8 minutes or until toasted and fragrant, stirring halfway through.
2. Coat 3 (9-inch) round cake pans with cooking spray. Line bottom of each pan with parchment paper; coat paper with cooking spray.
3. Whisk together flour and next 5 ingredients in a large bowl. Add eggs, oil, and vanilla, and stir just until dry ingredients are moistened. Fold in bananas, pineapple, and pecans. (Batter will be very thick, more like banana bread batter than cake batter.) Spoon batter into prepared pans.
4. Bake at 350° for 28 to 30 minutes. Cool in pans on a wire rack 10 minutes. Remove from pans to wire rack, and cool completely (about 30 minutes). Peel off and discard parchment paper.
5. Place 1 cake layer on a cake stand or serving plate. Top with one-fourth of frosting. Repeat procedure once. Top with remaining cake layer. Spread remaining frosting over top and sides of cake. Garnish, if desired.
Makes: 12 servings Hands-on Time: 30 min.
Total Time: 1 hr., 50 min., including frosting

cream cheese frosting

2 (8-oz.) packages cream cheese, softened
1 cup unsalted butter, softened
1 tsp. vanilla extract
2 cups powdered sugar, sifted

1. Place first 3 ingredients in the bowl of a heavy-duty electric stand mixer, and beat at medium speed using the paddle attachment until smooth. Gradually add powdered sugar, beating at low speed until blended after each addition. Beat at medium-high speed 3 minutes or until light and fluffy.
Makes: 5 cups Hands-on Time: 10 min. Total Time: 10 min.

lane cake

This iconic Southern cake, referenced in To Kill a Mockingbird, *has been around for more than 100 years. The airy cake layers get lighter with each additional sifting of flour. The potent liquor in the filling infuses the layers and makes the cake get better with time. Some versions have the edges enrobed in white frosting. I prefer this traditional version, with the filling dribbling down the sides. Start the filling first to give the raisins time to drink up the rum.*

Lane Cake Filling
Vegetable cooking spray
Parchment paper
3½ cups all-purpose soft-wheat flour (such as White Lily)
2 tsp. baking powder
⅛ tsp. salt
1 cup unsalted butter, softened
2 cups sugar, sifted
1 cup milk
1 tsp. vanilla extract
8 egg whites
1 wooden skewer

1. Prepare Lane Cake Filling through Step 2.
2. Preheat oven to 375°. Coat 2 (9-inch) round cake pans with cooking spray. Line bottom of each pan with parchment paper; coat paper with cooking spray.
3. Sift together flour, baking powder, and salt 5 times, sifting from one bowl to another as you work.
4. Place butter and sugar in the bowl of a heavy-duty electric stand mixer, and beat at medium speed until light and fluffy. Add flour mixture to butter mixture alternately with milk, beginning and ending with flour mixture. Beat at low speed until blended after each addition. Add vanilla, and beat just until blended.
5. Beat egg whites with an electric mixer at high speed until stiff peaks form. Gently fold egg whites into batter. Divide batter between prepared pans.
6. Bake at 375° for 30 minutes or until lightly golden. Cool cake in pans 10 minutes. Remove from pans to wire racks, and cool completely (about 1 hour). Peel off and discard parchment paper.
7. Meanwhile, continue to prepare filling as directed in Steps 3 through 5.
8. Place 1 cake layer on a cake stand or serving plate. Poke dozens of holes in top of cake using a wooden skewer, poking about halfway through cake and wiggling the skewer a little to widen the holes.
9. Slowly pour half of filling over cake, letting the filling soak in. Top with remaining cake layer. Poke holes into top cake layer with skewer, poking all the way through and again wiggling the skewer to widen the holes. Pour remaining filling over top cake layer. (Filling will run over sides of cake.) Let stand 1 hour before serving. Store, covered, in refrigerator.

Makes: 10 to 12 servings   Hands-on Time: 50 min.
Total Time: 7 hr., 30 min., including filling

lane cake filling

- 1 cup walnuts, chopped
- 1 cup golden raisins
- 1 cup dark rum
- 8 egg yolks
- 1 cup sugar
- ⅛ tsp. salt
- ½ cup unsalted butter, melted
- 1½ cups unsweetened medium-to-large-flake coconut (such as Bob's Red Mill Unsweetened Flaked Coconut)
- 1 tsp. vanilla extract

1. Preheat oven to 350°. Bake walnuts in a single layer in a shallow pan 6 to 8 minutes or until toasted and fragrant, stirring halfway through.
2. Combine raisins and rum. Cover and soak 4 to 24 hours.
3. Place egg yolks in a stainless-steel bowl, and beat at high speed with an electric mixer until fluffy. Add sugar and salt, and beat until very light yellow.
4. Pour water to depth of 1 inch in a medium saucepan. Bring to a boil over high heat; reduce heat to low, and maintain at a simmer.
5. Stir butter into egg mixture; place bowl over pan of simmering water, and cook, stirring constantly, until a candy thermometer registers 160° (about 10 minutes). Remove from heat; stir in raisins and rum, walnuts, coconut, and vanilla.

Makes: 4¼ cups **Hands-on Time: 20 min.** **Total Time: 4 hr., 30 min.**

priscilla's fresh peach pie (pictured on pages 254–255, top)

Priscilla Garrison taught school in my hometown. A truly gifted home cook, she is one of few who still insist on using only fresh, ripe peaches in pies. This recipe is an homage to her and that worthy but fading tradition. Once you taste the real thing, you'll know what you've been missing.

crust

2½ cups all-purpose soft-wheat flour (such as White Lily)
3 Tbsp. sugar
½ tsp. salt
1 cup cold unsalted butter, cut into ½-inch cubes
6 to 8 Tbsp. ice water

filling

2¼ lb. fresh peaches, peeled and sliced (about 4½ cups sliced)
¾ cup sugar
2 Tbsp. fresh lemon juice
¼ cup cornstarch
1 Tbsp. plus 1 tsp. almond paste

remaining ingredients

1 large egg, lightly beaten
2 Tbsp. sugar

1. Prepare Crust: Combine first 3 ingredients in a bowl; cut butter into flour mixture with a pastry blender or fork until crumbly. Sprinkle cold water, 1 Tbsp. at a time, over mixture in bowl; stir with a fork until dry ingredients are moistened. Shape into 2 balls; wrap in plastic wrap, and chill 30 minutes.
2. Prepare Filling: Combine peach slices and next 2 ingredients in a medium bowl. Whisk together cornstarch and ¼ cup liquid from peach mixture in a small bowl. Whisk in almond paste. Add cornstarch mixture to peach mixture, and stir until blended.
3. Uncover 1 dough ball. Roll into a 13-inch circle on a lightly floured surface. Fit into a 9-inch deep-dish pie plate; fold edges under, and crimp. Spoon peach mixture into piecrust. Cover and chill while you work with remaining dough ball.
4. Preheat oven to 425°. Roll remaining dough to ⅛-inch thickness on a lightly floured surface. Using the width of a ruler as a guide, cut dough into 9 (1-inch-wide) strips. Arrange strips in a lattice design over filling; gently press ends of strips into bottom piecrust to seal. Brush lattice lightly with egg; sprinkle with 2 Tbsp. sugar. Chill 10 minutes.
5. Place pie on a jelly-roll pan. Bake at 425° for 20 minutes. Reduce oven temperature to 350°, and bake 1 hour and 5 minutes, shielding edges with aluminum foil after 50 minutes to prevent excessive browning. Cool completely on a wire rack before serving (about 2 hours).

Makes: 8 servings Hands-on Time: 35 min. Total Time: 4 hr., 40 min.

pumpkin pie with brown sugar pecans

(pictured on page 254)

I love when the leaves are bright orange and deep red, but fall hasn't arrived until I've baked a pumpkin pie. The brown sugar-pecan topping on this one serves two purposes: It adds a terrific, nutty crunch and also cleverly conceals the cracks that sometimes form when pumpkin pie filling puffs and settles in the oven.

crust

1⅓ cups all-purpose flour
½ tsp. salt
½ cup shortening
4 to 6 Tbsp. ice water

topping

½ cup chopped pecans
¼ cup firmly packed light brown sugar

filling

1 (15-oz.) can pumpkin
⅔ cup firmly packed light brown sugar
½ cup half-and-half
3 large eggs
1 Tbsp. all-purpose flour
2 Tbsp. cane syrup
1 tsp. vanilla extract
½ tsp. salt
¼ tsp. ground nutmeg
⅛ tsp. ground cloves
⅛ tsp. ground cinnamon
⅛ tsp. ground allspice

1. Prepare Crust: Combine flour and salt; cut shortening into flour mixture with a pastry blender or fork until mixture resembles small peas. Sprinkle cold water, 1 Tbsp. at a time, over mixture in bowl; stir with a fork until dry ingredients are moistened. Shape dough into a ball; cover and chill 1 hour.
2. Preheat oven to 450°. Roll dough to ⅛-inch thickness on a lightly floured surface. Fit into a 9-inch pie plate; trim off excess pastry along edges. Fold edges under, and crimp. Line pastry with aluminum foil, and fill with pie weights or dried beans.
3. Bake at 450° for 8 minutes. Remove weights and foil; bake 3 minutes. Remove crust from oven to a wire rack. Reduce oven temperature to 350°.
4. Prepare Topping: Pulse pecans and brown sugar in a blender or food processor 4 times or until finely chopped.
5. Prepare Filling: Whisk together pumpkin and next 11 ingredients in a large bowl. Pour into prepared crust.
6. Bake at 350° for 30 minutes. Remove from oven, and top with pecan mixture. Bake 15 more minutes or until set. Cool completely on a wire rack (about 3 hours).
Makes: 8 servings **Hands-on Time: 25 min.** **Total Time: 5 hr., 20 min.**

chocolate-bourbon pecan pie

(pictured on pages 254-255, bottom)

Pecans suspended in a fudgy, bourbon-kissed filling are near perfection. This is one rich and over-the-top pie, so cut the slices small. A little goes a long way.

1⅓ cups all-purpose flour
½ tsp. salt
½ cup shortening
4 to 6 Tbsp. ice water
4 Tbsp. unsalted butter
6 oz. bittersweet chocolate baking bar
3 large eggs, lightly beaten
¾ cup sugar
½ cup light corn syrup
2 Tbsp. bourbon
1 tsp. vanilla extract
⅛ tsp. salt
2 cups pecans

1. Combine flour and ½ tsp. salt; cut shortening into flour mixture with a pastry blender or fork until mixture resembles small peas. Sprinkle cold water, 1 Tbsp. at a time, over mixture in bowl; stir with a fork until dry ingredients are moistened. Shape dough into a ball; cover and chill 45 minutes.
2. Preheat oven to 450°. Roll dough to ⅛-inch thickness on a lightly floured surface. Fit into a 9-inch pie plate; trim off excess pastry along edges. Fold edges under, and crimp. Line pastry with aluminum foil, and fill with pie weights or dried beans.
3. Bake at 450° for 8 minutes. Remove weights and foil; bake 6 more minutes. Remove from oven to a wire rack to cool. Reduce oven temperature to 350°.
4. Pour water to depth of 1 inch in a small saucepan, and bring to a boil over high heat; reduce heat to low, and maintain at a simmer. Combine butter and chocolate in a stainless-steel bowl. Place bowl over pan of simmering water, and cook, stirring frequently, 3 minutes or until melted. Remove from heat. Whisk in eggs and next 5 ingredients. Stir in pecans. Pour mixture into prepared crust.
5. Bake at 350° for 1 hour or until set and slightly puffed. Cool completely on a wire rack (about 1 hour).
Makes: 10 servings Hands-on Time: 20 min. Total Time: 3 hr., 25 min.

triple-nut skillet brittle (pictured on page 258)

I would eat so much brittle as a child that I can remember several occasions when my teeth actually stuck together for a few seconds. I love this version, which comes together in a skillet rather than a saucepan and doesn't require a candy thermometer. Just be sure to measure out all the ingredients before you start, and let the syrup turning the color of honey be your cue to work quickly.

Vegetable cooking spray
1 cup sugar
½ cup light corn syrup
½ cup roasted salted peanuts
½ cup roasted cashews
½ cup roasted macadamia nuts, chopped
2 Tbsp. unsalted butter
1 tsp. baking soda
½ tsp. fleur de sel (flaky sea salt)

1. Coat a 15- x 10-inch jelly-roll pan with cooking spray.
2. Stir together sugar, corn syrup, and ¼ cup water in a heavy 12-inch skillet over medium-high heat. (Do not use a nonstick skillet.) Bring to a rolling boil, stirring constantly. Cook 4 to 5 more minutes, stirring constantly. Stir in all nuts. Cook, stirring occasionally, 5 minutes or until syrup thickens and turns the color of honey.
3. Remove from heat, and quickly stir in butter and baking soda (mixture will bubble up). Stir until butter is fully incorporated. Pour onto prepared pan. Spread as thinly as desired, using 2 forks. (The forks snag the mixture better than a spoon, making it easier to stretch the brittle out to the pan edges. They do not leave tine marks.) Sprinkle with salt.
4. Cool completely (about 15 minutes). Break into large pieces by hand. Store in an airtight container.
Makes: about 1 lb. Hands-on Time: 20 min. Total Time: 40 min.

no-nuts divinity

No Southern candy has played a bigger role in my life than divinity. My grandmother Tom made it often, without a recipe in sight. She always added pecans, but I prefer it without nuts. I like to eat divinity without having to chew. I know now that divinity is not for the candy-making novice. You have to watch the clock, the thermometer, and the weather report. It will not set up if the humidity is too high, so wait for a dry, sunny day.

3 cups sugar
½ cup light corn syrup
2 egg whites, at room temperature
½ tsp. salt
1½ tsp. vanilla extract
Wax paper

1. Combine first 2 ingredients and ¾ cup water in a 2-qt. heavy saucepan. Bring to a rolling boil over medium heat without stirring; cook, brushing down any sugar crystals on sides of pan using a pastry brush dipped in hot water, until a candy thermometer registers 254° (about 19 minutes). Remove from heat.
2. Place egg whites and salt in the bowl of a heavy-duty electric stand mixer, and beat at high speed until stiff peaks form. With mixer running, slowly add half of hot syrup in a thin, steady stream, beating constantly at high speed (about 3 minutes).
3. Cook remaining half of syrup over medium heat until a candy thermometer registers 270° (soft crack stage; about 4 minutes). Slowly pour hot syrup and vanilla over egg white mixture in a thin, steady stream, beating constantly at high speed until mixture holds its shape and begins to lose its gloss (5 to 7 minutes).
4. Working very quickly, drop mixture onto wax paper using 2 stainless-steel spoons. Cool completely (about 10 minutes).

Makes: 1½ lb. Hands-on Time: 50 min. Total Time: 1 hr., 5 min.

mexican hot-chocolate refrigerator fudge

Making homemade fudge is as Southern as it gets. With a hint of cinnamon and a touch of spice, this refrigerator fudge is rich and satisfying for grown-ups—and easy enough for the children to help create.

Vegetable cooking spray
Parchment paper
1 (14-oz.) can sweetened condensed milk
1 Tbsp. brewed espresso or extra-strong brewed coffee
1 lb. high-quality bittersweet chocolate, chopped (about 2 cups)
3 Tbsp. unsalted butter
2 tsp. ground cinnamon
⅛ tsp. ground chipotle chile pepper
½ tsp. kosher salt

1. Coat an 8-inch square pan with cooking spray. Line bottom of pan with 1 sheet of parchment paper, allowing 2 inches to extend over sides; lightly spray parchment paper with cooking spray.
2. Pour water to depth of 1 inch into a 4-qt. saucepan; bring to a boil over high heat. Reduce heat to medium-low, and maintain at a simmer.
3. Stir together sweetened condensed milk and espresso in a medium-size stainless-steel bowl; stir in chocolate and butter. Place bowl over simmering pan of water, making sure bottom of bowl does not touch water. Cook, stirring constantly, 6 minutes or just until chocolate is melted and mixture is smooth. (Mixture will be thick.) Stir in cinnamon and chipotle chile pepper.
4. Transfer mixture to prepared pan, and smooth top with a rubber spatula. Sprinkle with salt. Chill 3 hours or until firm.
5. Lift fudge from pan, using parchment paper sides as handles. Cut into 25 squares. Store in an airtight container in refrigerator up to 1 week, or freeze up to 1 month.

Makes: 25 servings Hands-on Time: 20 min. Total Time: 3 hr., 25 min.

pecan tassies

These tiny pecan pies are almost too adorable to eat. My baby daughter has only a few words in her vocabulary, but she quickly applied two of them—"cute" and "nummy"—to pecan tassies. I first learned to place the pecans directly into the dough shells from my dear friend Virginia Willis. This method ensures each tassie gets an equal amount of pecans.

1¼ cups chopped pecans, divided
½ cup unsalted butter, softened
4 oz. cream cheese, softened
1 cup plus 2 Tbsp. all-purpose flour
⅛ tsp. salt
⅔ cup firmly packed light brown sugar
2 Tbsp. unsalted butter, melted
1 large egg, lightly beaten
1 tsp. vanilla extract
¼ tsp. salt

1. Preheat oven to 350°. Process ½ cup of the pecans in a blender or food processor until finely ground.
2. Place ½ cup butter and cream cheese in the bowl of a heavy-duty electric stand mixer, and beat at low speed until blended. Add flour, salt, and ground pecans; beat until blended.
3. Shape dough into 24 balls using lightly floured hands. Place 1 ball in each cup of 1 (24-cup) miniature muffin pan, and press dough on bottom and up sides of each cup to form shells. Arrange about 1 tsp. of the remaining chopped pecans in each shell.
4. Whisk together brown sugar and remaining ingredients. Spoon about 1 tsp. brown sugar mixture over pecans.
5. Bake at 350° for 22 minutes. Cool completely in pan on a wire rack (about 10 minutes).

Makes: 24 servings **Hands-on Time:** 30 min. **Total Time:** 1 hr.

peppermint wedding cookies

A woman in my hometown used her car to crush peppermint candies. I think of her each time I pull out the rolling pin and zip-top plastic bag to pulverize my own. This recipe tastes like a hybrid of a wedding cookie and a melt-away mint. The peppermint candy crumbs give a burst of refreshing sweetness with each bite.

1 cup unsalted butter, softened
½ cup powdered sugar, sifted
1 tsp. peppermint extract
2 cups all-purpose flour
½ tsp. salt
10 hard peppermint candies, crushed
½ cup powdered sugar
Parchment paper

1. Beat butter at medium speed with an electric mixer until creamy; gradually add ½ cup sifted powdered sugar and peppermint extract, beating well. Add flour and salt, beating until blended. Cover and chill dough 30 minutes.
2. Preheat oven to 350°. Place crushed peppermints in a bowl. Place ½ cup powdered sugar in a second bowl. Shape dough into 20 (1¼-inch) balls; place 1 inch apart on parchment paper-lined baking sheets.
3. Bake at 350° for 18 minutes or until bottoms are golden (tops will be pale). Immediately roll each cookie in crushed peppermints and then in powdered sugar. Generously sprinkle peppermints on top of each cookie, mounding slightly. (Peppermints will stick to cookies as they cool.) Cool completely on wire racks (about 30 minutes).
Makes: 20 cookies Hands-on Time: 20 min.
Total Time: 1 hr., 40 min.

pine nut blondies (pictured on page 266)

Graham cracker crust and pine nuts make the most sophisticated blondies ever. Pack these rich squares for tailgates, or wrap them individually to use as edible party favors.

1¼ cups graham cracker crumbs
⅓ cup melted unsalted butter
¼ cup granulated sugar
2 cups firmly packed light brown sugar
¾ cup unsalted butter
3 large eggs
2¼ cups all-purpose flour
2½ tsp. baking powder
½ tsp. salt
2 tsp. vanilla extract
1 cup pine nuts

1. Preheat oven to 350°. Line a 13- x 9-inch pan with aluminum foil, allowing 2 to 3 inches to extend over sides; lightly grease foil.
2. Combine graham cracker crumbs, melted butter, and granulated sugar in a bowl. Press mixture on bottom of prepared pan.
3. Cook brown sugar and ¾ cup butter in a heavy saucepan over medium heat, stirring constantly, 2 minutes or until butter melts.
4. Remove from heat. Add eggs, 1 at a time, to brown sugar mixture, stirring quickly after each addition. Combine flour, baking powder, and salt. Add to brown sugar mixture, whisking until mixture is blended and smooth. Stir in vanilla and pine nuts. Immediately pour batter over graham cracker crust.
5. Bake at 350° for 38 minutes. Cool blondies completely in pan on a wire rack (about 1 hour and 30 minutes). Lift blondies from pan, using foil sides as handles. Cut into 24 squares.
Makes: 2 dozen Hands-on Time: 20 min. Total Time: 2 hr., 28 min.

triple chocolate brownies (pictured on pages 266-267)

I love licking the spoon when I make brownies. Maybe that's why I prefer moist, fudgy brownies like these.

Parchment paper
½ cup bittersweet chocolate morsels
¼ cup semisweet chocolate morsels
2 Tbsp. milk chocolate morsels
¾ cup unsalted butter
1½ cups granulated sugar
3 large eggs
1 cup all-purpose flour
1 tsp. vanilla extract
⅛ tsp. salt
Powdered sugar (optional)

1. Preheat oven to 350°. Lightly grease a 9-inch square pan. Line bottom and sides with parchment paper, allowing 2 to 3 inches to extend over sides; lightly grease parchment paper.
2. Combine bittersweet chocolate and next 3 ingredients in a medium saucepan. Cook over medium heat, stirring constantly, 4 minutes or until melted. Remove from heat, and cool 1 minute. Whisk in granulated sugar. Add eggs, 1 at a time, whisking just until blended after each addition. Whisk in flour and next 2 ingredients. Pour into prepared pan.
3. Bake at 350° for 42 minutes. Cool completely in pan on a wire rack (about 30 minutes). Lift brownies from pan, using parchment paper sides as handles. Cut into 16 squares. Dust with powdered sugar, if desired.
Makes: 16 servings Hands-on Time: 15 min.
Total Time: 1 hr., 30 min.

table talk:
drop-leaf table
Few tables are as customizable as the drop-leaf table. These versatile and long-lived Southern favorites come in many sizes and can have rounded or square-edged leaves. Often used as side tables when the leaves are down, the tables very easily expand when needed. A hinged leg or brace swings out to support the leaf when it's fully extended.

Drop-leaf tables can be positioned, partly opened, at the ends of a larger dining room table or stand alone, fully unfurled, for extra seating. Whether antique or new, these smartly designed tables are decorative and functional pieces.

lemon icebox pie squares

This rich frozen lemon pie is made in a rectangular baking dish, making it easy to cut into squares. It has a thick and wonderful graham cracker crust. Lining the dish with foil makes for super-easy cutting.

18 graham cracker sheets
½ cup unsalted butter, melted
⅓ cup sugar
7 egg yolks
2 (14-oz.) cans sweetened condensed milk
1 Tbsp. lemon zest
1 cup fresh lemon juice (about 6 lemons)
½ tsp. vanilla extract
Sweetened whipped cream (optional)
Garnish: fresh mint sprigs

1. Preheat oven to 350°. Pulse graham cracker sheets in a food processor 3 to 4 times or until crackers resemble coarse sand. Add butter and sugar. Pulse until crumbs are moist.
2. Line an 11- x 7-inch baking dish with aluminum foil, allowing 2 to 3 inches to extend over sides. Lightly grease foil. Press cracker crumb mixture firmly on bottom of dish.
3. Whisk egg yolks until blended. Whisk in sweetened condensed milk and next 3 ingredients. Pour over crust.
4. Bake at 350° for 15 minutes or until slightly set. Cool completely on a wire rack (about 1 hour).
5. Cover with plastic wrap; freeze 8 to 24 hours. Lift pie from dish, using foil sides as handles. Remove foil; place pie on a cutting board. Let stand at room temperature 15 minutes; cut into squares. Serve with whipped cream, if desired. Garnish, if desired.
Makes: 8 to 10 servings   Hands-on Time: 15 min.
Total Time: 9 hr., 45 min.

peach ice cream

I can still hear the ice-cream machine humming away on the screened porch. Perfectly ripe peaches and loads of ice and salt transformed hot afternoons into magical summer fun when I was a kid. My sister and I would swim and play under the pecan trees while the grown-ups kept the machine churning. The minute our favorite hot-weather treat was ready, we'd dip our spoons straight into the machine. To this day, I still like my ice cream soft and right out of the churn.

2½ lb. ripe peaches, peeled and sliced (about 5 cups sliced)
2 cups half-and-half
1 cup heavy cream
1 cup milk
1½ cups sugar
6 egg yolks, lightly beaten
⅛ tsp. salt
¼ tsp. almond extract
Garnish: fresh basil sprigs

1. Process peaches in a blender or food processor until smooth, stopping to scrape down sides as needed.
2. Whisk together half-and-half and next 5 ingredients in a heavy saucepan; cook over medium heat, stirring constantly, 13 to 15 minutes or until mixture thickens and coats a spoon. (Do not boil.) Remove from heat. Pour into a bowl set atop a larger bowl filled with ice water. Add peach puree and almond extract, and whisk until mixture is cool. Discard ice water. Cover and chill mixture 4 hours.
3. Pour mixture into freezer container of a 1-gal. electric ice-cream maker, and freeze according to manufacturer's instructions. Garnish, if desired.
Makes: 2½ qt. Hands-on Time: 25 min. Total Time: 6 hr., 55 min.

Note: The total time for this recipe may vary, depending on your ice-cream maker.

raspberry-lime frozen pops

Leaving the raspberry seeds in the puree makes for an unexpected and fun crunch in these frozen pops. Pop molds vary in size, and if yours don't hold a full 4 ounces, you may end up with a little leftover puree. Use it as a cocktail base (add vodka and lemon-lime soda to taste), or drizzle it over ice cream, waffles, or pound cake.

½ cup sugar
6 cups fresh raspberries
¼ cup fresh lime juice (about 3 limes)
¼ tsp. vanilla extract
Garnish: fresh raspberries

1. Heat sugar and ½ cup water in a small saucepan over medium heat until sugar dissolves (about 3 minutes). Cool slightly (about 5 minutes).
2. Puree sugar syrup, raspberries, and next 2 ingredients in a blender until smooth, stopping to scrape down sides as needed.
3. Pour mixture into 10 (4-oz.) plastic pop molds (about ⅓ cup mixture in each). Top with lids of pop molds, and insert craft sticks, leaving 1½ to 2 inches of each sticking out. Freeze 6 hours or until sticks are solidly anchored and pops are completely frozen. Garnish, if desired.

Makes: 10 servings Hands-on Time: 10 min. Total Time: 6 hr., 10 min.

watermelon sherbet

Cold, juicy watermelons turn July, even in Georgia, into a refreshing experience. We float them in swimming pools, pickle their rinds, and make use of every second they're in season. We even freeze them for an extra chilly treat.

8 cups chopped watermelon (about 3 lb.)
1 cup half-and-half
¾ cup sugar
Garnish: mint sprigs

1. Process watermelon in a blender until pureed, stopping to scrape down sides as needed. Transfer 4½ cups puree to a large bowl. Reserve any remaining watermelon puree for another use. (Or grab a straw for a cook's treat.) Whisk in half-and-half and sugar.
2. Pour mixture into freezer container of a 1½-qt. electric ice-cream maker, and freeze according to manufacturer's instructions. Transfer to an airtight container, and freeze 4 to 5 hours. Let stand at room temperature 5 to 10 minutes before serving. Garnish, if desired.

Makes: 1½ qt. Hands-on Time: 20 min. Total Time: 5 hr.

Note: The total time for this recipe may vary, depending on your ice-cream maker.

my southern table

My favorite memories around the table are those that bring laughter: the cranberry sauce that inevitably gets left in the refrigerator every holiday or the pasta that somehow ends up in my son's hair. My parents love to tell how, as a toddler, I fell asleep at Thanksgiving dinner, my gentle head bobs ultimately giving way to a face full of mashed potatoes.

Growing up in Oklahoma, I was in charge of setting the table and arranging the food for holiday dinners. I enjoyed being Mother's helper. The more I helped, the earlier I was able to sneak a sample of the good stuff or find the best piece of turkey. My parents were adamant that we enjoy at least one meal each day together as a family. With my gymnastics training regimen, that often meant 9 p.m. dinners. Even at that late hour, we were able to connect in ways both small and hugely important.

One evening in the summer of 1993 stands out very clearly to me. I had just finished an incredible stretch, with five Olympic medals at the 1992 Barcelona Olympics followed by All-Around Gold at the 1993 World Championship competition. I was dealing with injuries and burnout, however, and I announced to my parents and coach at our dining table that I intended to retire from the sport I love. Instead of arguing, my coach calmly asked me why. I soon realized it was not about the sport as much as it was about the lack of goals I had. Goals kept me going—a new skill to master, a score to achieve. That evening changed the course of my athletic career and taught me an important life lesson.

Now I am able to share that memory and create new ones with my husband and son. While we don't have a lavish meal every night, our time in the kitchen and around the dining table, at the breakfast bar, or on our sunny Florida patio is special. While we catch up and decompress from hectic work schedules, our 2-year-old son stands with a dishtowel wrapped around his waist, mixing, pouring, and talking about his favorite foods. I hope he'll grow to know that the profound conversations, the friendships nurtured, and the love spread around it are what transform a dining table into a dining experience.

Shannon Miller

Olympic gymnast, health-and-fitness advocate

Winner of seven Olympic and nine World Championship gymnastics medals

Barcelona '92
In 3qt. pan, put: 2c sugar
stick butter
1/2 c milk
1 1/2 cup Butter
3 eggs 1/2 t. salt
1 tsp. Vanilla
Bake at 350°

paper napkins & extra leaves

menus for everyday meals and entertaining

Weekend Brunch with Neighbors

Invite the neighbors over for a relaxing morning visit. Make the coffee cake the night before, and sip a mimosa while the eggs cook. Tie a ribbon on extra jars of preserves for guests to enjoy at home.

Mimosas (equal parts orange juice and Champagne)

Apple-Glazed Sausages and Vidalias, page 30

Cheddar Scrambled Eggs, page 18

Brown-Butter Coffee Cake with Peaches and Blueberries, page 39

Fig Preserves, page 79, with soft cheese

BIG BREAKFAST *with Soul*

When a hearty start to the morning is just what the doctor ordered, go all out and dig in to one of the South's best-kept secrets: chicken and waffles. Serve the chicken on the side of the waffle or pile it sky-high on top. Slather the waffles with softened butter, and drizzle it all with a sweet dose of sorghum syrup. Add hot sauce if you like.

Buttermilk and Brown Sugar Waffles, page 35

Real Buttermilk Fried Chicken, page 104

Sorghum syrup, softened butter, hot sauce

Fresh fruit

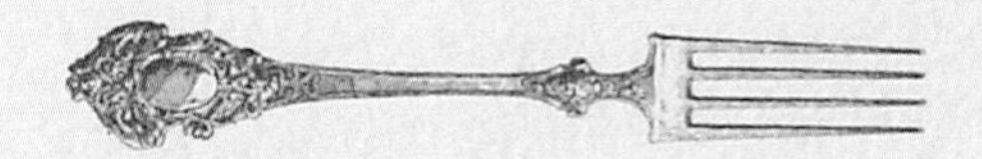

picnic in the country

Pack a picnic, and enjoy the outdoors in all its glory. Wrap utensils in napkins, and tie with raffia for a pretty and easy way to set the outdoor "table." Transport and serve the lemonade in pint jars, so all they need is a little ice when you arrive.

raspberry lemonade, page 66

divine pimiento cheese, page 52, with crackers

chèvre and cucumber stars, page 51

ham salad croissants, page 189

pickled okra, page 83

pine nut blondies, page 268

SUNDAY LUNCH

Enjoying a big Sunday lunch is practically a birthright in the South. Make the pound cake and deviled eggs, and marinate the chicken the day before. Have the family over after church, and enjoy the most special meal of the week.

Sugar Sweet Tea, page 66

Bacon Deviled Eggs, page 52

Real Buttermilk Fried Chicken, page 104

Herbed Buttermilk Biscuits, page 165

Heirloom Tomato Salad, page 205

Pound Cake from Heaven, page 243

Rainy Day Lunch

Staying in and enjoying a grilled cheese on a rainy day is one of my favorite things. Start the chowder as the clouds roll in.

Grilled Cheese and Tomato Sandwiches, page 186

Rich Corn Chowder, page 174

Afternoon Tailgate

In Georgia Bulldog country, we know a good tailgate. Pull out the julep cups, and start the day off right. The rest of these kick-off-worthy recipes can be made ahead and packed for a feast on campus.

Blackberry Mint Julep, page 65

Hot Pepper Jelly, page 83, with cream cheese and crackers

Spiced and Smoked Boston Butt, page 119

Sweet Potato Biscuits, page 163

Chocolate-Bourbon Pecan Pie, page 256

SUPPER *on a School Night*

Make weeknights easy with a homemade casserole that can be pulled together earlier in the day or even on the weekend. Use a rotisserie chicken for a shortcut, and make the kids extra happy with cornbread sticks.

Chicken and Wild Rice with Pecans, page 146

Cucumber and Tomato Salad, page 202

Cornbread Sticks, page 150

Fresh fruit

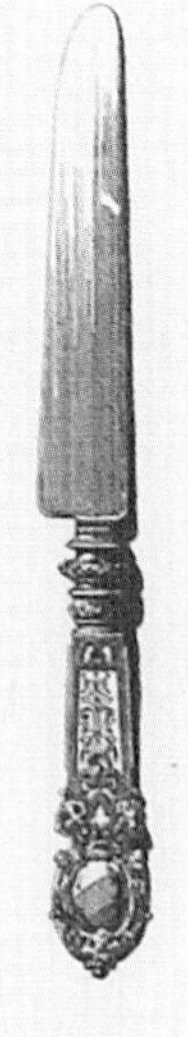

backyard lowcountry boil

Cover the table with newspaper, and bring the coast closer. Make the coleslaw and the pie squares a day ahead. Fry up the hush puppies as the water heats for the boil.

lowcountry boil, page 88

spicy coleslaw, page 203

buttermilk hush puppies stuffed with pimiento cheese, page 151

lemon icebox pie squares, page 271

Dinner Party with Friends

Hosts who aren't tied to the stove all evening give the best dinner parties. The day before, stir together the spread, trim the asparagus, bake the phyllo dough for the napoleons, and peel the shrimp. When the doorbell rings, you'll have a few finishing touches and plenty of time to catch up.

Vidalia Spread, page 58, with crackers

Atlantic Shrimp and Grits, page 93

Marinated Asparagus and Pecan Salad, page 213

Sliced tomatoes

Berry Napoleons with Buttermilk Whipped Cream, page 234

SUMMER SOLSTICE COOKOUT

Celebrate the longest day of the year with friends in the backyard. Make the sangría and the salads the day before. Fire up the grill while the guests mingle, and let the ice cream churn during supper.

Summer Fruit Sangría, page 63

English Pea and Radish Salad, page 202

New Potato Salad with Dill, page 209

White Barbecued Chicken, page 107

Grilled Summer Squash with Rosemary, page 226

Peach Ice Cream, page 272

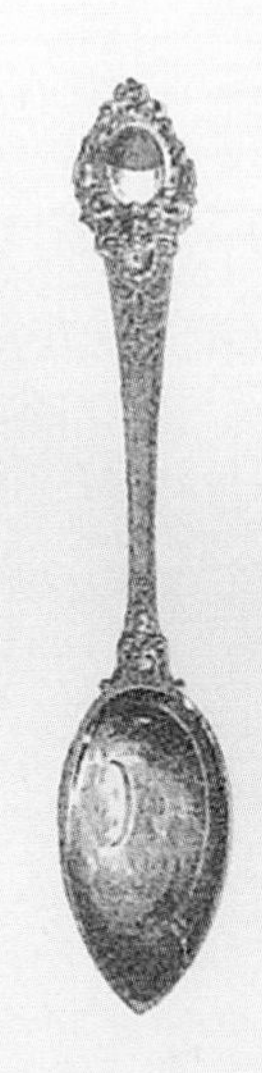

ELEGANT HOLIDAY MEAL

A holiday is made even more memorable when you gather around the table for an impressive meal. Make it relaxing, too, by finishing half the menu the day before. Ice the cake and make the soup while the ham cooks in the oven.

Creamy Butternut Squash Soup, page 176

Pecan, Bourbon, and Cane Syrup Ham, page 115

Stuffed Baked Vidalias, page 229

Swiss Chard with Bacon Butter, page 217

Cloverleaf Yeast Rolls, page 155

Raspberry-Lime Coconut Cake, page 246

NEW YEAR'S DAY *Lunch*

Keep tradition alive even as you turn the calendar page. With black-eyed peas for prosperity, cornbread for gold, greens for money, and pork for luck, it's going to be a big year. Make the collard greens and soak the black-eyed peas on New Year's Eve.

Hoppin' John Bake, page 139

Old-Fashioned Collard Greens, page 214

Butter-Fried Pork Chops with Nutmeg, page 113

Family Cornbread, page 145

Oxmoor House
VP, Publishing Director: Jim Childs
Editorial Director: Leah McLaughlin
Creative Director: Felicity Keane
Senior Brand Manager: Daniel Fagan
Senior Editor: Rebecca Brennan
Managing Editor: Rebecca Benton

Around the Southern Table
Author and Recipe Creator: Rebecca Lang
Editor: Nichole Aksamit
Project Editor: Emily Chappell
Designer: Felicity Keane
Director, Test Kitchen: Elizabeth Tyler Austin
Assistant Directors, Test Kitchen: Julie Christopher, Julie Gunter
Recipe Developers and Testers: Wendy Ball, R.D.; Victoria E. Cox; Stefanie Maloney; Callie Nash; Leah Van Deren
Recipe Editor: Alyson Moreland Haynes
Food Stylists: Margaret Monroe Dickey, Catherine Crowell Steele
Production Manager: Theresa Beste-Farley

Contributors
Compositor: Carol Damsky
Recipe Developers and Testers: Tamara Goldis, Erica Hopper, Tonya Johnson, Kyra Moncrief, Kathleen Royal Phillips
Photographer: Jennifer Davick
Food Stylist: Marian Cooper Cairns
Photo Stylist: Lydia DeGaris Pursell
Recipe Editor: Ashley Leath
Copy Editors: Carmine B. Loper, Barry Smith
Proofreaders: Donna Baldone, Norma Butterworth-McKittrick
Indexer: Mary Ann Laurens
Interns: Morgan Bolling; Jessica Cox, R.D.; Mackenzie Cogle; Laura Hoxworth; Susan Kemp; Emily Robinson; Ashley White

Southern Living®
Editor: M. Lindsay Bierman
Creative Director: Robert Perino
Managing Editor: Candace Higginbotham
Art Director: Chris Hoke
Executive Editors: Rachel Hardage Barrett, Jessica S. Thuston
Food Director: Shannon Sliter Satterwhite
Test Kitchen Director: Rebecca Kracke Gordon
Senior Writer: Donna Florio
Senior Food Editor: Mary Allen Perry
Recipe Editor: JoAnn Weatherly
Assistant Recipe Editor: Ashley Arthur
Test Kitchen Specialist/Food Styling: Vanessa McNeil Rocchio
Test Kitchen Professionals: Norman King, Pam Lolley, Angela Sellers
Senior Photographers: Ralph Lee Anderson, Gary Clark, Art Meripol
Photographers: Robbie Caponetto, Laurey W. Glenn
Photo Research Coordinator: Ginny P. Allen
Senior Photo Stylist: Buffy Hargett
Editorial Assistants: Cory Bordonaro, Marian Cooper, Stephanie Granada, Pat York

Time Home Entertainment Inc.
Publisher: Richard Fraiman
VP, Strategy & Business Development: Steven Sandonato
Executive Director, Marketing Services: Carol Pittard
Executive Director, Retail & Special Sales: Tom Mifsud
Director, Bookazine Development & Marketing: Laura Adam
Executive Publishing Director: Joy Butts
Finance Director: Glenn Buonocore
Associate General Counsel: Helen Wan

metric equivalents

The recipes that appear in this cookbook use the standard U.S. method for measuring liquid and dry or solid ingredients (teaspoons, tablespoons, and cups). The information in the following charts is provided to help cooks outside the United States successfully use these recipes. All equivalents are approximate.

Metric Equivalents for Different Types of Ingredients

A standard cup measure of a dry or solid ingredient will vary in weight depending on the type of ingredient. A standard cup of liquid is the same volume for any type of liquid. Use the following chart when converting standard cup measures to grams (weight) or milliliters (volume).

Standard Cup	Fine Powder *(ex. flour)*	Grain *(ex. rice)*	Granular *(ex. sugar)*	Liquid Solids *(ex. butter)*	Liquid *(ex. milk)*
1	140 g	150 g	190 g	200 g	240 ml
¾	105 g	113 g	143 g	150 g	180 ml
⅔	93 g	100 g	125 g	133 g	160 ml
½	70 g	75 g	95 g	100 g	120 ml
⅓	47 g	50 g	63 g	67 g	80 ml
¼	35 g	38 g	48 g	50 g	60 ml
⅛	18 g	19 g	24 g	25 g	30 ml

Useful Equivalents for Liquid Ingredients by Volume

¼ tsp							=	1 ml		
½ tsp							=	2 ml		
1 tsp							=	5 ml		
3 tsp	=	1 Tbsp			=	½ fl oz	=	15 ml		
		2 Tbsp	=	⅛ cup	=	1 fl oz	=	30 ml		
		4 Tbsp	=	¼ cup	=	2 fl oz	=	60 ml		
		5⅓ Tbsp	=	⅓ cup	=	3 fl oz	=	80 ml		
		8 Tbsp	=	½ cup	=	4 fl oz	=	120 ml		
		10⅔ Tbsp	=	⅔ cup	=	5 fl oz	=	160 ml		
		12 Tbsp	=	¾ cup	=	6 fl oz	=	180 ml		
		16 Tbsp	=	1 cup	=	8 fl oz	=	240 ml		
		1 pt	=	2 cups	=	16 fl oz	=	480 ml		
		1 qt	=	4 cups	=	32 fl oz	=	960 ml		
						33 fl oz	=	1000 ml	=	1 l

Useful Equivalents for Dry Ingredients by Weight

(To convert ounces to grams, multiply the number of ounces by 30.)

1 oz	=	¹⁄₁₆ lb	=	30 g
4 oz	=	¼ lb	=	120 g
8 oz	=	½ lb	=	240 g
12 oz	=	¾ lb	=	360 g
16 oz	=	1 lb	=	480 g

Useful Equivalents for Length

(To convert inches to centimeters, multiply the number of inches by 2.5.)

1 in					=	2.5 cm		
6 in	=	½ ft			=	15 cm		
12 in	=	1 ft			=	30 cm		
36 in	=	3 ft	=	1 yd	=	90 cm		
40 in					=	100 cm	=	1 m

Useful Equivalents for Cooking/Oven Temperatures

	Fahrenheit	Celsius	Gas Mark
Freeze water	32° F	0° C	
Room temperature	68° F	20° C	
Boil water	212° F	100° C	
Bake	325° F	160° C	3
	350° F	180° C	4
	375° F	190° C	5
	400° F	200° C	6
	425° F	220° C	7
	450° F	230° C	8
Broil			Grill

index

Beef
Burgers, Pimiento Cheese-Stuffed, 195
Meatloaf, Stuffed, 120
Pot Roast with Baby Vegetables, Oven, 124
Standing Rib Roast, Coffee-Crusted, 125
Steak, Crispy Country-Fried, 122
Beverages
Lemonade, Raspberry, 66
Mint Julep, Blackberry, 65
Sangría, Summer Fruit, 63
Tea, Sugar Sweet, 66
Biscuits
Angel Biscuits, 157
Cat-head Biscuits with Tomato Gravy, 159
Drop-and-Cut Biscuits, 162
Herbed Buttermilk Biscuits, 165
Itsy-Bitsy Cream Cheese Biscuits, 156
Sweet Potato Biscuits, 163
Yogurt-and-Cream Biscuits, Nathalie's, 160
Breads. *See also* Biscuits, Cornbreads.
Beignets with Buttermilk, 43
Country Ham-and-Cheese Biscuit Bread, 153
French Toast, Pound Cake, 23
Muffins, Ginger and Peach, 36
Pudding, Bacon-and-Swiss Bread, 149
Rolls, Cloverleaf Yeast, 155
Waffles, Buttermilk and Brown Sugar, 35
Brunswick Stew, Sweet and Smoky Grilled, 182

Cakes
Caramel Cake, Six-Layer, 244
Coffee Cake, Honey-Pecan, 40
Coffee Cake with Peaches and Blueberries, Brown-Butter, 39
Hummingbird Cake, 249
Lane Cake, 250
Pound Cake from Heaven, 243
Raspberry-Lime Coconut Cake, 246
Candies
Brittle, Triple-Nut Skillet, 257
Divinity, No-Nuts, 259
Fudge, Mexican Hot-Chocolate Refrigerator, 260
Casseroles
Blue Crab Casserole, 141
Chicken and Wild Rice with Pecans, 146
Green Bean Casserole, Garden, 130
Hoppin' John Bake, 139
Macaroni with Five Cheeses, 142
Oysters with Spinach, Creamed, 135
Sweet Potato Casserole, All Things, 132
Winter Greens-and-Butternut Squash Gratin, Virginia's, 143
Cheese
Pimiento Cheese, Buttermilk Hush Puppies Stuffed with, 151
Pimiento Cheese, Divine, 52
Pimiento Cheese-Stuffed Burgers, 195
Chicken
Bog, Chicken, 102
Dressing, Chicken and, 145
Dumplings, Chicken and Rolling Pin, 180
Fried Chicken, Real Buttermilk, 104
Livers, Cornmeal-Crusted Chicken, 107
Pot Pie, Puffed Chicken, 136
White Barbecued Chicken, 107
Wild Rice with Pecans, Chicken and, 146
Condiments
Beets with Allspice and Ginger, Pickled, 80
Butter, Homemade Basil, 30
Canning Instructions, General, 73
Chowchow, Green Tomato, 80
Chutney, Clementine and Cranberry, 75
Jam, Country Ham, 19
Jam, Spiced Tomato Refrigerator, 69
Jam, Strawberry-Basil, 69
Jelly, Hot Pepper, 83
Jelly, Scuppernong, 76
Pickled Okra, 83
Preserves, Blueberry and Lemon, 70
Preserves, Fig, 79
Relish, Corn, 191
Salsa, Summer, 222
Spread, Vidalia, 58
Vinegar, Hot Pepper, 225
Cornbreads
Family Cornbread, 145
Lace Cornbread, 167
Sticks, Cornbread, 150
Cornish Hens with Lemons and Creamy Grits, Roasted, 101

Desserts. *See also* Cakes, Candies.
Blondies, Pine Nut, 268
Brownies, Triple Chocolate, 269
Cobbler, Peach and Blueberry, 241
Cobblers, Blackberry One-Biscuit Mini, 235
Cookies, Peppermint Wedding, 265
Curd, Lime, 247
Filling, Lane Cake, 251
Frosting, Caramel, 245
Frosting, Cream Cheese, 249
Frosting, Seven-Minute Coconut, 247
Ice Cream, Peach, 272
Napoleons with Buttermilk Whipped Cream, Berry, 234
Pie, Chocolate-Bourbon Pecan, 256
Pie, Priscilla's Fresh Peach, 252
Pie Squares, Lemon Icebox, 271
Pie with Brown Sugar Pecans, Pumpkin, 253
Pops, Raspberry-Lime Frozen, 274
Pudding Brûlée, Sorghum Syrup Rice, 237
Pudding, Real Banana, 238
Sherbet, Watermelon, 274
Tassies, Pecan, 262
Duck Breasts, Peach-Glazed, 113

Eggs
Breakfast in a Skillet, 21
Deviled Eggs, Bacon, 52
Scrambled Eggs, Cheddar, 18

Fish and Seafood
Blue Crab Casserole, 141
Catfish, Crispy, 94
Catfish Sandwiches with Corn Relish, 191
Flounder, Pecan-Crusted, 94
Lowcountry Boil, 88
Oyster Stew, Simple Southern, 172
Oysters with Spinach, Creamed, 135
Salmon Croquettes, 97
Scallops, Brown Sugar-Bacon Wrapped, 48
Shrimp and Grits, Atlantic, 93
Shrimp Bisque, Georgia, 179
Shrimp, Skillet Barbecued, 91
Shrimp with Sweet-and-Spicy Peach Sauce, Coconut Fried, 89
Trout Wrapped in Bacon, Stuffed, 97
Fritters with Summer Salsa, Corn, 222

Gravy, Country Ham with Redeye, 18
Gravy, Tomato, 159
Grits
Blue Cheese Grits, 116
Creamy Grits, 101
Puffy Grits, 32
Stone-Ground Grits with Homemade Basil Butter, 30
White Cheese Grits, 98

Hoppin' John Bake, 139
Hush Puppies Stuffed with Pimiento Cheese, Buttermilk, 151

Peaches
Cobbler, Peach and Blueberry, 241
Ice Cream, Peach, 272
Pie, Priscilla's Fresh Peach, 252
Poblanos, White Cheese Grits-Stuffed, 98
Pork
Bacon, Sweet Candied, 23
Boston Butt, Spiced and Smoked, 119
Chops with Nutmeg, Butter-Fried Pork, 113
Ham, Pecan, Bourbon, and Cane Syrup, 115
Ham with Redeye Gravy, Country, 18
Roast with Blue Cheese Grits, Peppered Pork, 116
Sausage and Cheese Soufflé, 29
Sausages and Vidalias, Apple-Glazed, 30

Salads and Salad Dressings
Beet and Chèvre Salad, 206
Chicken-and-Avocado Salad, Fried, 108
Chicken Salad, Roasted, 210
Coleslaw, Spicy, 203
Cucumber and Tomato Salad, 202
English Pea and Radish Salad, 202
Ham Salad Croissants, 189
Heirloom Tomato Salad, 205
Jalapeño Dressing, 108
Marinated Asparagus and Pecan Salad, 213
New Potato Salad with Dill, 209
Rice Salad, Carolina Gold, 209
Sandwiches
BLTs, Double, 195
Catfish Sandwiches with Corn Relish, 191
Croissants, Ham Salad, 189
Egg Sandwiches, Over-the-Top, 27
Fried Green Tomato Sandwiches, 185
Grilled Cheese and Tomato Sandwiches, 186
Hot Brown Sandwiches, Kentucky, 192
Open-Faced Meatloaf Sandwiches, 196
Po'boys, Fried Oyster, 188
Stars, Chèvre and Cucumber, 51
Sauces
Gorgonzola Sauce, Sweet Potato Chips with, 56
Red Bell Pepper Sauce, 55
Rémoulade Dipping Sauce, 61
Southern Ranchero Sauce, 98
Sweet-and-Spicy Peach Sauce, Coconut Fried Shrimp with, 89
Vinegar Sauce, 119
Sides
Carrots, Turnip Roots, and Vidalias, Roasted, 218
Cauliflower Gratin, Roasted, 131
Corn, Creamed Silver Queen, 221
Greens-and-Butternut Squash Gratin, Virginia's Winter, 143
Greens, Old-Fashioned Collard, 214
Okra, Whole Fried, 222
Pickles with Rémoulade Dipping Sauce, Fried, 61
Pink-Eyed Purple Hull Peas, Mimi's, 225
Squash Blossoms, Lemon-and-Cheese-Stuffed, 226
Squash Soufflé, Down-Home, 133
Squash with Rosemary, Grilled Summer, 226
Swiss Chard with Bacon Butter, 217
Tomatoes with Red Bell Pepper Sauce, Fried Green, 55
Vidalias, Stuffed Baked, 229
Soups
Bisque, Georgia Shrimp, 179
Butternut Squash Soup, Creamy, 176
Caramelized Vidalia Soup with Crispy Sage, 175
Chowder, Rich Corn, 174
Tomato-and-Roasted Red Pepper Soup with Cheddar Croutons, 173
Stew, Simple Southern Oyster, 172
Stew, Sweet and Smoky Grilled Brunswick, 182
Sweet Potato Chips with Gorgonzola Sauce, 56

Turkey, Bacon-Covered Roasted, 110

bibliography

Anderson, Jean. *A Love Affair with Southern Cooking.* New York: William Morrow, 2007.

Aronson, Joseph. *The Encyclopedia of Furniture.* New York: Crown Publishers, Inc., 1965.

Bitterman, Mark. *Salted: A Manifesto on the World's Most Essential Mineral, with Recipes.* Berkeley: Ten Speed Press, 2010.

Burroughs, Paul H. *Southern Antiques.* New York: Bonanza Books, 1967.

Dupree, Nathalie. *New Southern Cooking.* New York: Alfred A. Knopf, Inc., 1986.

Egerton, John. *Southern Food: At Home, on the Road, in History.* New York: Alfred A. Knopf, Inc., 1987.

Lang, Robert W., and Glen D. Huey. *Furniture in the Southern Style.* Cincinatti: Popular Woodworking Books, 2011.

Parker, Philip M. *Fashionables: Webster's Quotations, Facts and Phrases.* San Diego: Icon Group International Inc., 2009.

von Drachenfels, Suzanne. *The Art of the Table: A Complete Guide to Table Setting, Table Manners, and Tableware.* New York: Simon & Schuster, 2000.

acknowledgments

I find peace and comfort around the table mostly because of the people who always pull up a chair. My husband, Kevin, and my sweet children, Camden and Adair, give me joy beyond expression and have all become professional taste testers. My parents, Mandy and William Dopson, supported every step necessary for me to succeed in the kitchen. I could not do what I do without Mama here and ready to fill in when I'm covered up with work.

My agent, Carole Bidnick, championed this book into reality and encouraged me along the way. Nathalie Dupree gave me a start so many years ago and is now a cherished friend. She has mentored me, loved me, and taught me all the way from student to colleague.

My friends and family loaned me equipment, brainstormed ideas, and helped in countless ways: Meghan Garrard; Catherine Hardman; Sheila Snead; Suzanne Kilgore; Brooke Stortz; Mary DeLoach; Suzanne Rutledge; Melissa Halbach; my sister, Natalie Schweers; Taylor and Jeff Miller; my sister-in-law, Valery Hall; Donna Means; and Wendell Brock.

Jay Reardon shared his expertise and his library. My mother-in-law, Linda Lang, remains my No. 1 bookseller and a great help to me. Thanks to Celia Barrs and John Cooper, I was able to test recipes with the freshest and finest vegetables. Dink NeSmith kept our pantry and freezer stocked with sorghum syrup and quail. Wayne Tatum sent vegetables from South Georgia. Emily Robinson helped immeasurably with a refreshing work ethic. Abbey Warren ran all over town and allowed me to stay in and cook. Dick Parker shared his time and generosity.

Nathalie Dupree, Damon Lee Fowler, and Jean Anderson offered a wealth of Southern culinary and historical knowledge. Mary Moore gave me a job years ago and opened the door to all things food in Atlanta. Thank you to Wendy Allen, Jim Brams, and The Cook's Warehouse family for everything. I am grateful for Virginia Willis's friendship, guidance, and pep talks.

Jennifer Davick, Marian Cooper Cairns, and Lydia DeGaris Pursell shared their immense talent and created photographs that are nothing short of breathtaking. I have always dreamed of having my name on a book this pretty.

Thank you to my editor, Nichole Aksamit, for jumping in and taking off, and to Emily Chappell, Ashley Leath, and Barry Smith for their attention to detail. I am incredibly indebted to everyone at Oxmoor House and *Southern Living* who had faith in me and my work: Jim Childs, Susan Dobbs, Daniel Fagan, Felicity Keane, Becky Brennan, Lindsay Bierman, Helen Todd, Kristen Bryan, and Frank Craige.

Thanks, too, to Rucker Place in Birmingham for lending us a fine porch and to Henhouse Antiques in Birmingham for helping us locate and photograph many of the rare tables and treasured tabletop pieces featured in this book. Special thanks to Virginia Willis and Gena Berry in Atlanta, who helped us capture the elusive beaten biscuit brake.

about the author

Rebecca Lang is a food writer, cooking instructor, and a ninth-generation Southerner. Born and raised in South Georgia, she is author of *Quick-Fix Southern, Mary Mac's Tea Room,* and *Southern Entertaining for a New Generation.*

She and her cooking have been featured in more than 50 nationally televised *Southern Living* food segments and in publications such as *The Atlanta Journal-Constitution,* the *Houston Chronicle,* and *Glamour* and *Fitness* magazines.

A former assistant food editor at Oxmoor House, she earned a journalism degree from the University of Georgia and a culinary arts degree from Johnson & Wales University, and apprenticed with Southern cooking legend Nathalie Dupree.

She serves as a contributing editor for *Southern Living* magazine and MyRecipes.com, teaches cooking classes across America, and writes a blog at www.rebeccalangcooks.com that has been featured on the James Beard Foundation Blog, *Delights and Prejudices*, and noted in *Food News Journal*'s Best of the Blogs.

She resides in Athens, Georgia, with her husband, Kevin; their children, Camden and Adair; and their snuggly Cavalier King Charles Spaniel, Miss Bea.